EVALUATION OF
COMPETENCE TO
STAND TRIAL

BEST PRACTICES IN FORENSIC MENTAL HEALTH ASSESSMENT

Series Editors

Thomas Grisso, Alan M. Goldstein, and Kirk Heilbrun

Series Advisory Board

Paul Appelbaum, Richard Bonnie, and John Monahan

Titles in the Series

Foundations of Forensic Mental Health Assessment, *Kirk Heilbrun, Thomas Grisso, and Alan M. Goldstein*

Criminal Titles

Evaluation of Competence to Stand Trial, *Patricia A. Zapf and Ronald Roesch*

Evaluation of Criminal Responsibility, *Ira K. Packer*

Evaluation of Capacity to Confess, *Alan M. Goldstein and Naomi Goldstein*

Evaluation of Sexually Violent Predators, *Philip H. Witt and Mary Alice Conroy*

Evaluation for Risk of Violence in Adults, *Kirk Heilbrun*

Jury Selection, *Margaret Bull Kovera and Brian L. Cutler*

Evaluation for Capital Sentencing, *Mark D. Cunningham*

Eyewitness Identification, *Brian L. Cutler and Margaret Bull Kovera*

Civil Titles

Evaluation of Capacity to Consent to Treatment, *Scott Y.H. Kim*

Evaluation for Substituted Judgment, *Eric Y. Drogin and Curtis L. Barrett*

Evaluation for Civil Commitment, *Debra Pinals and Douglas Mossman*

Evaluation for Harassment and Discrimination Claims, *William Foote and Jane Goodman-Delahunty*

Evaluation of Workplace Disability, *Lisa D. Piechowski*

Juvenile and Family Titles

Evaluation for Child Custody, *Geri S.W. Fuhrmann*

Evaluation of Juveniles' Competence to Stand Trial, *Ivan Kruh and Thomas Grisso*

Evaluation for Risk of Violence in Juveniles, *Robert Hoge and D.A. Andrews*

Evaluation for Child Protection, *Kathryn Kuehnle, Mary Connell, Karen S. Budd, and Jennifer Clark*

Evaluation for Disposition and Transfer of Juvenile Offenders, *Randall T. Salekin*

EVALUATION OF COMPETENCE TO STAND TRIAL

PATRICIA A. ZAPF

RONALD ROESCH

OXFORD
UNIVERSITY PRESS

2009

OXFORD
UNIVERSITY PRESS

Oxford University Press, Inc., publishes works that further
Oxford University's objective of excellence
in research, scholarship, and education.

Oxford New York
Auckland   Cape Town   Dar es Salaam   Hong Kong   Karachi
Kuala Lumpur   Madrid   Melbourne   Mexico City   Nairobi
New Delhi   Shanghai   Taipei   Toronto

With offices in
Argentina   Austria   Brazil   Chile   Czech Republic   France   Greece
Guatemala   Hungary   Italy   Japan   Poland   Portugal   Singapore
South Korea   Switzerland   Thailand   Turkey   Ukraine   Vietnam

Copyright © 2009 by Oxford University Press, Inc.

Published by Oxford University Press, Inc.
198 Madison Avenue, New York, New York 10016
www.oup.com

Oxford is a registered trademark of Oxford University Press

Library of Congress Cataloging-in-Publication Data

Zapf, Patricia A., 1971–
Evaluation of competence to stand trial / Patricia A. Zapf, Ronald Roesch.
p. ; cm. — (Best practices in forensic mental health assessment)
Includes bibliographical references and index.
ISBN 978-0-19-532305-4
1. Forensic psychiatry. 2. Competency to stand trial. I. Roesch, Ronald,
1947– II. Title. III. Series.
[DNLM: 1. Forensic Psychiatry—methods—Canada.
2. Forensic Psychiatry—methods—United States. 3. Mental Competency—
Canada. 4. Mental Competency—United States. W 740 Z35e 2008]
RA1151.Z37 2008
614'.1—dc22

2008026688

9 8 7 6 5 4 3 2 1

Printed in the United States of America
on acid-free paper

About Best Practices in Forensic Mental Health Assessment

The recent growth of the fields of forensic psychology and forensic psychiatry has created a need for this book series describing best practices in forensic mental health assessment (FMHA). Currently, forensic evaluations currently are conducted by mental health professionals for a variety of criminal, civil, and juvenile legal questions. The research foundation supporting these assessments has become broader and deeper in recent decades. Consensus has become clearer on the recognition of essential requirements for ethical and professional conduct. In the larger context of the current emphasis on "empirically supported" assessment and intervention in psychiatry and psychology, the specialization of FMHA has advanced sufficiently to justify a series devoted to best practices. Although this series focuses mainly on evaluations conducted by psychologists and psychiatrists, the fundamentals and principles offered would also apply to evaluations conducted by clinical social workers, psychiatric nurses, and other mental health professionals.

This series describes "best practice" as empirically supported (when the relevant research is available), legally relevant, and consistent with applicable ethical and professional standards. Authors of the books in this series identify the approaches that seem best, while incorporating what is practical and acknowledging that best practice represents a goal to which the forensic clinician should aspire rather than a standard that can always be met. The American Academy of Forensic Psychology assisted the editors in enlisting the consultation of board-certified forensic psychologists specialized in each topic area. Board-certified forensic psychiatrists were also consultants on many of the volumes. Their comments on the manuscripts helped to ensure that the methods described in these volumes represent a generally accepted view of best practice.

The series' authors were selected for their specific expertise in a particular area. At the broadest level, however, certain general principles apply to all types of forensic evaluations. Rather than repeat those fundamental principles in every volume, the series offers them in the first volume, *Foundations of Forensic Mental Health Assessment*. Reading the first book followed by a specific topical book will provide the reader both the general principles that the specific topic shares with all forensic evaluations and those that are particular to the specific assessment question.

The specific topics of the 19 books were selected by the series editors as the most important and oft-considered areas of forensic assessment conducted by mental health professionals and behavioral scientists. Each of the 19 topical books is organized according to a common template. The authors address the applicable legal context, forensic mental health concepts, and empirical foundations and limits in the "Foundation" part of the book. They then describe preparation for the evaluation, data collection, data interpretation, and report writing and testimony in the "Application" part of the book. This creates a fairly uniform approach to considering these areas across different topics. All authors in this series have attempted to be as concise as possible in addressing best practice in their area. In addition, topical volumes feature elements to make them user-friendly in actual practice. These elements include boxes that highlight especially important information, relevant case law, best-practice guidelines, and cautions against common pitfalls. A glossary of key terms is also provided in each volume.

We hope the series will be useful for different groups of individuals. Practicing forensic clinicians will find succinct, current information relevant to their practice. Those who are in training to specialize in forensic mental health assessment (whether in formal training or in the process of respecialization) should find helpful the combination of broadly applicable considerations presented in the first volume together with the more specific aspects of other volumes in the series. Those who teach and supervise trainees can offer these volumes as a guide for practices to which the trainee can aspire. Researchers and scholars interested in FMHA best practice may find researchable ideas, particularly on topics that have received insufficient research attention to date. Judges and attorneys with questions about FMHA best practice will find these books relevant and concise. Clinical and forensic administrators who run agencies, court clinics, and hospitals in which litigants are assessed may also use some of the books in this series to establish expectancies for evaluations performed by professionals in their agencies.

We also anticipate that the 19 specific books in this series will serve as reference works that help courts and attorneys evaluate the quality of forensic mental health professionals' evaluations. A word of caution is in order, however. These volumes focus on best practice, not what is minimally acceptable legally or ethically. Courts involved in malpractice litigation, or ethics committees or licensure boards considering complaints, should not expect that materials describing best practice easily or necessarily translate into the minimally acceptable professional conduct that is typically at issue in such proceedings.

This volume addresses best-practice standards in conducting competence to stand trial evaluations. Referrals to assess a defendant's fitness for trial is the most frequently requested type of forensic evaluation. The significance of the forensic mental health professional's opinion cannot be overstated, in terms of both the implications for the integrity of the criminal legal process that is to follow, and for the outcome of the trial and the impact of the verdict on the defendant's life. Zapf and Roesch recognize the importance of these evaluations. This book will serve as a guide for forensic mental health professionals to conduct assessments that are legally relevant, consistent with professional ethics, and use empirically grounded methodology, and to present their findings in an objective, thorough, data-based fashion.

Alan M. Goldstein
Kirk Heilbrun
Thomas Grisso

Acknowledgments

We would like to thank the series editors, Alan M. Goldstein, Kirk Heilbrun, and Thomas Grisso for providing us the opportunity to write this book and for their helpful suggestions and guidance along the way. In addition, we are appreciative of the comments and suggestions of the external reviewers, Richard Frederick and Charles Patrick Ewing. Finally, as always, we owe a debt of gratitude for the support of our significant others, Rob and Kim. Thank you!

Contents

FOUNDATION

The Legal Context | 1

One of the primary foundations of criminal law is that all defendants have a right to a fair trial. In addition, criminal defendants must be capable of actively participating in their defense. However, for some defendants, mental health problems or cognitive deficits hinder their ability to participate in the proceedings. To preserve the dignity and integrity of judicial proceedings, and to protect defendants' due process rights, the notion of trial competency has evolved. The evaluation of trial competency is arguably the most common type of involvement of forensic mental health professionals in the criminal justice system. As Golding (1992) noted, "more defendants are evaluated for competency and more resources expended for their evaluation, adjudication, and treatment than for any other class of forensic activities" (p. 77). Indeed, it is estimated that between 2% and 8% of all felony defendants are referred for competency evaluations (Bonnie, 1992b; Golding, 1993; Hoge, Bonnie, Poythress, & Monahan, 1992), accounting for nearly 60,000 or more competency evaluations annually in the United States (Bonnie & Grisso, 2000).

This chapter provides a review of the legal context for competency evaluations. In subsequent chapters, we will review forensic mental health concepts (Chapter 2), the research on those being evaluated for trial fitness and the assessment procedures used to evaluate competency (Chapter 3), and the evaluation process (Chapters 4–7), including preparing for and conducting the evaluation, interpreting the results, writing reports, and providing expert testimony.

Historical Overview

Adoption of the Doctrine From English Common Law

The legal context for competence to stand trial (CST) in the United States can be traced back to English common law dating from at least the 17th century. In the 18th century, Sir William Blackstone wrote:

> If a man in his sound memory commits a capital offence, and before arraignment for it, he becomes mad, he ought not to be arraigned for it: because he is not able to plead to it with that advice and caution that he ought. And if, after he has pleaded, the prisoner becomes mad, he shall not be tried: for how can he make his defence? If, after he be tried and found guilty, he loses his senses before judgment, judgment shall not be pronounced; and if, after judgment, he becomes of nonsane memory, execution shall be stayed: for peradventure, says the humanity of the English law, had the prisoner been of sound memory, he might have alleged something in stay of judgment or execution. (Blackstone, 1769, p. 24)

Blackstone's *Commentaries on the Laws of England* (1765–1769) was influential in shaping law and legal procedures in both England and the United States. Perhaps the first American defendant found *Incompetent to Stand Trial* (IST) was Richard Lawrence, who attempted to assassinate President Andrew Jackson in 1835 (*United States v. Lawrence*, 1835). After being deemed incompetent, Lawrence spent the rest of his life in jails and mental hospitals. Late in the 19th century, the case of *Youtsey v. United States* (1899) extended and helped shape the notion that certain defendants should be barred from trial. Youtsey was epileptic, which had delayed his trial for several months. The trial court denied his motion that his epilepsy impaired his memory and affected his ability to communicate facts to his lawyer. He was convicted, but the Court of Appeals reversed his conviction, holding that it was "doubtful whether the accused was capable of appreciating his situation, and of intelligently advising his counsel as to his defense" (p. 947), noting that "it is not 'due process of law' to subject an insane person to trial upon an indictment involving liberty or life" (p. 941).

"Presence" at Trial, Fairness, and Accuracy

The competency doctrine evolved at a time when defendants were not provided with the right to assistance of counsel and, in many cases, were expected to present their defense alone and unaided. It is believed by some that the competency doctrine arose in response to the problem of defendants who stood mute rather than entering a required plea. In these instances, the court would be required to determine whether the defendant was "mute of malice" or "mute by visitation of God" (Robertson, 1925). Those who were found to be maliciously mute were subjected to torture, whereas those mute "by visitation of God" (which included both those who were deaf and unable to speak as well as those who were considered "lunatic") were spared. Thus, even early on there was recognition that more than mere physical presence was required for a defendant to confront his accusers and present a defense.

Various legal commentators have delineated several principles underlying the rationale for the competency doctrine. The Group for the Advancement of Psychiatry (1974) summarized four underlying principles, including

1. to safeguard the accuracy of any criminal adjudication;
2. to guarantee a fair trial;
3. to preserve the dignity and integrity of the legal process; and
4. to be certain that the defendant, if found guilty, knows why he is being punished (p. 889).

Bonnie (1992b) explained that allowing only those who are competent to proceed protects the dignity, reliability, and autonomy of the proceedings. The underlying rationale, then, concerns both the protection of the defendant as well as the protection of the state's interest in fair and reliable proceedings.

Competence to Stand Trial and Its Relation to Adjudicative Competence

Although the term *competence to stand trial* (CST) has been used for centuries, there has begun a recent shift in terminology to reflect the fact that the vast majority of cases are plead out before getting to trial and that the issue of "trial" competency can be raised at any stage of the proceedings—from arrest to verdict to sentencing. Bonnie (1992b), Poythress and colleagues (1999, 2002), and others have suggested the use of terms such as *adjudicative competence* or *competence to proceed* to better reflect the reality of this doctrine. Throughout this book, we will use the terms competence to stand trial, adjudicative competence, and competence to proceed interchangeably.

Legal Standards

Dusky and *Drope*

The legal standards for adjudicative competence clearly define competency as an issue of a defendant's present mental status and functional abilities as they relate to participation in the trial process. This distinguishes competency from *criminal responsibility*, which refers to a defendant's mental state at the time of the offense. In an extremely brief decision, the U.S. Supreme Court established the modern day standard for CST in *Dusky v. United States* (1960). Citing a recommendation of the Solicitor General, the Court held that,

> It is not enough for the district judge to find "the defendant [is] oriented to time and place and [has] some recollection of events," but that the "test must be whether he has sufficient present ability to consult with his lawyer with a reasonable degree of rational understanding—and whether he has a rational as well as factual understanding of the proceedings against him." (p. 402)

The *Dusky* decision provides little detail or elaboration on these criteria. How should we define, and of course assess, a sufficient ability to consult with a lawyer? What constitutes a reasonable degree of rational understanding? How does a rational understanding differ from a factual understanding? Of course, the answers to these questions cannot be found simply in the wording of the legal criterion. Rather, they must come from examining how the law is actually applied and interpreted (both by legal scholars as well as by the courts). The components of the legal standards for competency will be further elaborated here and in Chapter 2.

Kruh and Grisso (2009) provide a closer analysis of some of the terms used in the *Dusky* test to help clarify its meaning:

- *Sufficient* ability and *reasonable* understanding specify that CST does not require complete and fully unimpaired functioning. *Reasonable* also implies relativity in relation to the context. That is, abilities must be better developed for complex cases than for simple cases.

- *Present* ability specifies that CST is explicitly a "current mental state question." Therefore, by definition, CST is independent of retrospective forensic mental health questions, such as mental state at the time of the offense. However, *present* is generally accepted to include the immediate future, as the trial process will typically proceed for some brief period after a determination of competency.

- *Ability* connotes that the test seeks to identify individuals who are unable to function adequately, not those who are unfamiliar with appropriate functioning or those who choose not to participate adequately.

- The distinction between *factual* and *rational* understanding communicates that more than a concrete, rote understanding is required to possess CST.

- The *and* linking the two prongs indicates that both components are necessary. (p. 14, italics in original)

Fifteen years after *Dusky,* the U.S. Supreme Court in *Drope v. Missouri* (1975) appeared to elaborate slightly on the competency standard by including the notion that the defendant must be able to "assist in preparing his defense" (p. 171). Legal scholars, such as Bonnie (1993), as well as the American Bar Association Criminal Justice Mental Health Standards (1989), indicated that *Drope* added another prong to *Dusky* by requiring

CASE LAW
Dusky v. United States (1960)

- Established the modern day standard for competence to stand trial

- Defendant must have sufficient present ability to consult with a lawyer with a reasonable degree of rational understanding, as well as factual understanding of the proceedings

CASE LAW

Drope v. Missouri (1975)

- Required that the defendant be able to assist in preparing his defense and added another prong—"otherwise assist"—to the Dusky standard

- Held that the court should be aware of any changes in the defendant's condition that might raise questions about his competency at any point during the trial proceedings

that defendant be able to "otherwise assist with his defense" (ABA, 1989, p. 170). Similarly, the addition of this "otherwise assist" prong to the *Dusky* standard has been affirmed in cases such as *United States v. Duhon* (2000).

State Statutes

Every state has adopted the *Dusky* standard for competency, either verbatim or with minor revision. A review of state competency statutes indicated that at least five states (Alaska, Florida, Illinois, New Jersey, Utah) have also expanded or articulated the *Dusky* standard to include specific functional abilities (Zapf, 2002). Since the definition of competency varies by state, the evaluator must be sure to consult the relevant competency statutes and definitions before proceeding with the evaluation of a defendant's competency.

Apart from the definition or standard for competency, most state statutes provide little information about the nature of the evaluation and the report to the court; however, some states, such as Florida and Utah, provide considerable direction. Utah is perhaps the most specific about its expectations for the information that should be contained in the report. These include the criteria that follow from *Dusky*, as well as details about such issues as the ability to manifest appropriate courtroom behavior, to testify relevantly if applicable, and whether medication is necessary and, if so, what impact it might have on the defendant's demeanor, affect, and ability to participate in the proceedings (Utah Code Annotated, 2002).

BEST PRACTICE

Consult the relevant statutes, as definitions of competency and directions for the evaluation and report vary by state.

The Utah statute also directs evaluators to specify treatment for defendants thought to be incompetent, as well as assess their ability to provide *informed consent* to treatment. In Canada, a defendant is considered unfit (incompetent) to stand trial if he is

> unable on account of mental disorder to conduct a defence at any stage of the proceedings before a verdict is rendered or to instruct counsel to do so, and, in particular, unable on account of mental disorder to (a) understand the nature or object of the proceedings (b) understand the possible consequences of the proceedings, or (c) communicate with counsel. (Criminal Code of Canada, S.2, 1992)

Unlike the situation in the United States, wherein each state has its own competency statute and standard, this standard applies to all of Canada. One final note: The Canadian standard is nearly identical to the standard for competency used in Federal courts in the United States (see United States Code Annotated, Title 18, Part III, chapter 13, section 4241).

Case Law

In addition to state statutes, such as Utah's more detailed guidelines for evaluating competency, case law offers some elaboration and interpretation of *Dusky*.

In *Wieter v. Settle* (1961), the U.S. District Court for the Western District of Missouri determined that it was improper to further detain a defendant who had been charged with a misdemeanor offense and held for 18 months for *competence restoration* since prosecution was no longer probable. In delivering the court's opinion, Chief Judge Ridge delineated a series of eight functional abilities related to *Dusky* that a defendant must possess to be competent:

1. that he has mental capacity to appreciate his presence in relation to time, place, and things;
2. that his elementary mental processes be such that he apprehends (i.e., seizes and grasps with what mind he has) that he is in a Court of Justice charged with a criminal offense;
3. that there is a Judge on the Bench;
4. a Prosecutor present who will try to convict him of a criminal charge;

CASE LAW

Wieter v. Settle

(1961)

● Delineated a series of
eight functional
abilities related to
Dusky that a defendant
must possess to be
competent

5. that he has a lawyer (self-employed or
   Court-appointed) who will undertake to
   defend him against that charge;

6. that he will be expected to tell his lawyer
   the circumstances, to the best of his mental ability, (whether colored or not by
   mental aberration) the facts surrounding
   him at the time and place where the law
   violation is alleged to have been
   committed;

7. that there is, or will be, a jury present to
   pass upon evidence adduced as to his guilt
   or innocence of such charge; and

8. he has memory sufficient to relate those
   things in his own personal manner. (p. 320)

The U.S. Court of Appeals considered the relevance of amnesia to adequate participation in legal proceedings in *Wilson v.
United States* (1968). The court, in *Wilson,* delineated six factors
that must be considered:

1. the extent to which the amnesia affected the defendant's
   ability to consult with and assist his lawyer.

2. the extent to which the amnesia affected the defendant's
   ability to testify in his own behalf.

3. the extent to which the evidence in suit could be extrinsi-
   cally reconstructed in view of the defendant's amnesia. Such
   evidence would include evidence relating to the crime itself,
   as well as any reasonable possible alibi.

4. the extent to which the government assisted the defendant
   and his counsel in that reconstruction.

5. the strength of the prosecution's case. Most important here
   will be whether the government's case is such as to negate
   all reasonable hypotheses of innocence. If there is any substantial possibility that the accused could, but for his amnesia, establish an alibi or other defense, it should be
   presumed that he would have been able to do so.

CASE LAW

Wilson v. United States (1968)

● Delineated six factors that need to be considered for evaluating competency

● Related the specific deficits of the defendant to the legal context

6. any other facts and circumstances which would indicate whether or not the defendant had a fair trial. (pp. 463–464)

The *Wilson* factors clearly specify a functional approach to evaluating competency, in which the specific deficits of a defendant would be related to the legal context. We will elaborate on this approach in Chapter 2.

Competence to Waive Counsel and Plead Guilty

All defendants are provided the constitutional right to assistance of counsel; however, defendants may choose to waive this right and represent themselves (to appear *pro se*). This raises the question of whether competence to waive counsel should be evaluated separately from CST. Cases such as Colin Ferguson's cast considerable doubt on court decisions to allow certain defendants to represent themselves (Perlin, 1996). Colin Ferguson, a 37-year-old native of Jamaica who was clearly paranoid and mentally disturbed, shot and killed six people and wounded 19 others on a Long Island Rail Road commuter train in December 1993. Ferguson fired his defense attorney, who had intended to pursue an insanity defense, and decided to represent himself, using the defense that a White perpetrator stole his gun and was responsible for the shootings, despite numerous eyewitnesses to the contrary. On the basis of the Supreme Court's opinion in *Godinez* (discussed later), Ferguson was considered competent to waive his right to counsel (and proceed *pro se*). His trial is said to have made a mockery of the court system and has been characterized as a sham and a charade (Perlin, 1996).

Should there be a different, perhaps higher, standard for evaluating competency in cases in which the defendant waives counsel? What about those cases, such as that of Theodore Kaczynski, in which the defendant wishes to appear *pro se* in a capital case? It is also the case that most defendants do not actually go to trial, since plea bargaining accounts for the vast majority of dispositions of criminal cases. Again, should there be a different standard for evaluating competence to plead guilty? Many clinicians and researchers have argued that these are different abilities and that a defendant might be competent to stand trial but not competent to waive counsel or enter a guilty plea (Whittemore, Ogloff, & Roesch, 1997; see Zapf & Roesch, 2005a for a detailed discussion of this issue). Court decisions have been mixed on this issue with some (e.g., *Sieling v. Eyman,* 1973) holding that the standards are not the same and that there should be a higher standard for some rights, such as pleading guilty. The U.S. Supreme Court considered the issue of whether a higher standard should apply for waiving counsel or pleading guilty in *Godinez v. Moran* (1993). The defendant, Moran, after being found competent to stand trial, discharged his lawyers, entered a plea of guilty to three counts of murder, and was then sentenced to death. He appealed, arguing that although he had been found competent to stand trial, he was not competent to waive his right to counsel and represent himself. The U.S. Supreme Court rejected this argument and held that the standard for various types of competency (i.e., competence to plead guilty, to waive counsel, and to stand trial) should be considered the same. Justice Thomas wrote for the majority:

> A defendant who stands trial is likely to be presented with choices that entail relinquishment of the same rights that are relinquished by a defendant who pleads guilty. . . . all criminal defendants—not merely those who plead guilty—may be required to make important decisions once criminal proceedings have been initiated. And while the decision to plead guilty is undeniably a profound one, it is no more complicated than the sum total of decisions that a defendant may be called upon to make during the course of a trial. . . . Nor do we think that a defendant who waives his right to the assistance of counsel must be more competent than a defendant who does not, since there is no reason to believe that the decision to waive counsel requires an appreciably higher level of mental functioning than the decision to waive other constitutional rights. (p. 2686)

This decision appeared at odds with researchers and legal scholars, who had argued that different evaluation criteria would be appropriate for the various legal situations that a defendant might face (Bonnie, 1992b, 1993; Roesch & Golding, 1980). Justice Thomas also noted that,

> Requiring that a criminal defendant be competent has a modest aim: It seeks to ensure that he has the capacity to understand the proceedings and to assist counsel. While psychiatrists and scholars may find it useful to classify the various kinds and degrees of competence, and while States are free to adopt competency standards that are more elaborate than the Dusky formulation, the Due Process Clause does not impose these additional requirements. (p. 2687)

In his dissent, Justice Blackmun noted that the "majority's analysis is contrary to both common sense and long-standing case law" (p. 2691). Noting that prior Supreme Court cases have "required competency evaluations to be specifically tailored to the context and purpose of a proceeding" (p. 2694), Justice Blackman reasoned that competency cannot be considered apart from its specific legal context, that "A person who is 'competent' to play basketball is not thereby 'competent' to play the violin" (p. 2694), and thus "competency for one purpose does not necessarily translate to competency for another purpose." He also commented that,

> The standard for competence to stand trial is specifically designed to measure a defendant's ability to "consult with counsel" and to "assist in preparing his defense." A finding that a defendant is competent to stand trial establishes only that he is capable of aiding his attorney in making the critical decisions required at trial or in plea negotiations. The reliability or even relevance of such a finding vanishes when its basic premise—that counsel will be present—ceases to exist. The question is no longer whether the defendant can proceed with an attorney, but whether he can proceed alone and uncounseled. (p. 2694)

The *Godinez* decision has been criticized by legal scholars (e.g., Perlin, 1996). It remains unclear the extent to which this decision actually affects either evaluations or determinations of competency. Some have argued that the decision may elevate the

CASE LAW

Godinez v.

Moran (1993)

● U.S. Supreme Court held that the standard for various types of competency (competence to stand trial, competence to waive counsel, competence to plead guilty) should be the same.

● Other legal scholars have argued that different evaluation criteria for competency is appropriate for different legal contexts.

standard for competency, since the initial evaluation must take into account all of the decision-making abilities required at all stages of the proceedings, including waiving counsel, pleading guilty, and representing oneself, and not simply whether a defendant has a basic understanding of the arrest and legal proceedings and is able to communicate with counsel (see Grisso, 2003; Melton, Petrila, Poythress, & Slobogin, 2007). What seems clear, however, is that the *Dusky* standard is the constitutional minimum to be applied, regardless of the specific legal context, and that a defendant's decision-making abilities appear to be encompassed within this standard.

As this book goes to press, a recent decision by the U. S. Supreme Court in *Indiana v. Edwards* (2008) appears to redefine the *Godinez* decision and provide a framework for clinicians who are evaluating whether a defendant has the capacity for self-representation. Ahmad Edwards was charged with attempted murder, battery with a deadly weapon, criminal recklessness, and theft after he tried to steal a pair of shoes from a department store. When he was discovered, he shot at a security officer and wounded a bystander. He was found incompetent and committed for treatment. Following seven months of treatment, he was found competent but several months later he was again found incompetent and was recommitted for treatment. Following eight months of treatment, he was found competent. Edwards' trial began nearly one year after this determination of competency. Just prior to trial, Edwards asked to represent himself, asking for a continuance in order to proceed *pro se*. The court refused and Edwards was convicted of criminal recklessness and theft but the jury failed to reach a verdict on the charges of attempted murder and battery. The State decided to retry Edwards on these two charges, and again Edwards asked to represent himself. The court denied his request and Edwards was represented by counsel at his retrial, where he was convicted of both remaining counts.

Edwards appealed, arguing that the denial of his request to represent himself deprived him of his constitutional right of self-representation. The Indiana Supreme Court also considered the case and affirmed the Appeals Court decision, noting that precedent, particularly *Faretta* and *Godinez*, required the State to allow Edwards to represent himself. The U.S. Supreme Court, at Indiana's request, agreed to consider whether the Constitution requires the trial court to allow self-representation.

The Court acknowledged that *Faretta* affirms a constitutional right to proceed without counsel when a criminal defendant voluntarily and intelligently elects to do so, but the Court added that the right is not absolute, and the Edwards case requires a consideration of whether mental illness limits this right. Of course, the Court had considered the issue of competence and self-representation in *Godinez*, where (as we have discussed at length in this chapter) it was decided that there should not be a higher standard of competency for a defendant to waive the right of self-representation or to enter a guilty plea. On its face, the decision in *Godinez* would appear to suggest that if Edwards were competent to proceed with counsel, he would also be competent to represent himself. However, the Court in Edwards rejected this interpretation, arguing that in *Godinez* the issue was whether the defendant had the ability to proceed on his own simply to enter a guilty plea, not whether the defendant had the capacity to represent himself at trial.

The *Edwards* Court considered the issue of whether a State, in the case of a criminal defendant who meets the *Dusky* standard of competence to stand trial, can limit a criminal defendant's right of self-representation by requiring that the defendant be represented by counsel at trial. The Court answered in the affirmative when a defendant lacks the mental capacity to conduct a trial defense unless represented. The Court cited an American Psychiatric Association brief, submitted in this case, which argued that mental illness could impair a defendant's ability to engage in the expanded role required for self-representation even in cases where the defendant could proceed to trial with representation. Thus, the *Edwards* decision makes clear that the standard for competence may indeed vary in certain limited instances. At first glance, this appears to be inconsistent with the precedence established in *Godinez*, but the Court expressly addressed this by noting that,

> *Godinez* provides no answer here because that defendant's ability to conduct a defense at trial was expressly not an issue in that case . . . and because the case's constitutional holding that a State may *permit* a gray-area defendant to represent himself does not tell a State whether it may *deny* such a defendant the right to represent himself at trial. (p. 2, italics in original)

The *Edwards* decision establishes that competence to proceed *pro se* requires a higher level of competence than competence to stand trial, but is unclear exactly how that would be determined. It also places a high premium on preserving the dignity of the courtroom and the fairness of the trial. The decision notes that a right of self-representation would not affirm the dignity of a defendant who lacks mental capacity to conduct a defense without assistance of counsel, commenting that given a "defendant's uncertain mental state, the spectacle that could well result from his self-representation at trial is at least as likely to prove humiliating as ennobling" (p. 11).

In his dissent, Justice Scalia calls this decision extraordinarily vague. He notes that Edwards disagreed with his lawyers about how to present his case at trial. Edwards wanted a self-defense argument, while his lawyers wished to focus on lack of intent.

CASE LAW

Indiana v. Edwards (2008)

- U.S. Supreme Court held that the Constitution does not forbid States from insisting upon representation by counsel for those competent enough to stand trial but who suffer from mental illness to the point where they are not competent to conduct trial proceedings by themselves.

- The decision leaves unclear the standard to be used for competence to proceed *pro se* versus competence to stand trial.

While Scalia comments that he would have likely been convicted anyway, the Court erred in holding that a defendant who is competent to stand trial does not have the constitutional right to self-representation. Justice Scalia is also critical of the Court's concern with the dignity of the proceedings. He writes "Once the right of self-representation for the mentally ill is a sometime thing, trial judges will have every incentive to make their lives easier . . . by appointing knowledgeable and literate counsel" (p. 11 of dissent).

Thus, in light of the Supreme Court's decision in *Edwards*, what are the implications for evaluations of competence to stand trial wherein the defendant is requesting self-representation? At present, it appears too early to tell how various courts will consider this issue or the criteria that various states may adopt. We may, however, be able to ascertain some clue as to how this issue will be considered by examining the amicus briefs submitted in *Edwards*.

A number of *amici* submitted briefs in *Edwards*. Two briefs, in particular, are especially relevant when attempting to provide guidance to evaluators asked to consider a defendant's competence to stand trial without the assistance of counsel. The American Bar Association (ABA) submitted a brief in support of the petitioner (Indiana) wherein it was argued that the ABA's Criminal Justice Standards on Mental Health and the Special Functions of the Trial Judge provide a useful template for determining competency in this context. In its brief, the ABA highlighted that Standard 6–3.6 of the ABA Standards for Criminal Justice: Special Functions of the Trial Judge recommends that, before allowing a defendant to proceed without the assistance of counsel, trial judges determine that the defendant

   (i)   has been clearly advised of the right to the assistance of counsel, including the right to the assignment of counsel when the defendant is so entitled;

  (ii)   is capable of understanding the proceedings; and

 (iii)   has made an intelligent and voluntary waiver of the right to counsel.

The reader will note that this does not appear to deviate from the decision of the Supreme Court in *Godinez*. The ABA brief, however, goes on to elaborate that,

> if the court possesses 'a good faith doubt of the mental competence of the defendant to waive counsel or to represent himself or herself,' ABA Standard for Mental Health 7–5.3 recommends that the trial judge order a pretrial mental evaluation. Based on the results of that evaluation, the judge should determine whether the defendant has:
>
>> the present ability to knowingly, voluntarily, and intelligently waive the constitutional right to counsel, to appreciate the consequences of the decision to proceed without representation by counsel, to comprehend the nature of the charge and proceedings, the range of applicable punishments, and any additional matters essential to a general understanding of the case. (Standard 7–5.3(b))
>
> If the defendant lacks these abilities, Standard 7–5.3(a) provides that the court should not permit the defendant to proceed without the assistance of counsel. (Brief of the ABA as *amicus curiae* supporting petitioner in *Indiana v. Edwards*, pp. 8–9)

The American Psychiatric Association (APA) and the American Academy of Psychiatry and the Law (AAPL) submitted a joint brief in support of neither party wherein it was argued that the underlying capabilities relevant for self-representation are "generally extensions of assessments already embraced within the inquiries typically made for assessing competency to stand trial" (p. 27). The APA/AAPL brief also argued that since it has been determined that evaluations of CST are essentially high in reliability and validity, then these expanded evaluations of competency for self-representation should be reliable and valid as well. In essence, the APA/AAPL brief asserted a functional approach to the assessment of competency wherein the defendant's capabilities must be considered in light of the competence-related abilities required within the specific context[A]. The APA/AAPL brief noted that,

> In short, inquiries into decision-making and cognitive/communication capabilities are already part of the reliable assessment of competency to stand trial. Such inquiries, however, must be specific to the tasks involved, and those tasks are substantially expanded for a *pro se* defendant. What is required in this context, therefore, is a significant extension of inquiries already being made (albeit in a narrower focus) for the threshold assessment of competency to stand trial. (p. 33)

Thus, in evaluating competence to stand trial, the evaluator should be careful to consider whether the defendant is to proceed with or without the assistance of counsel. In those cases where the defendant is to proceed *pro se*, an evaluation of the expanded abilities required for self-representation should occur and a description of the degree of congruence/incongruence between the required abilities and the defendant's capabilities presented to the court.

Competency Procedures

Raising the Issue

Legal procedures are well-established to ensure that defendants are competent to proceed. In *Pate v. Robinson* (1966), the U.S. Supreme Court held that the competency issue must be raised by any officer of the court (defense, prosecution, or judge) if there is a *bona fide* doubt as to a defendant's competence. The threshold for establishing a *bona fide* doubt is low, and most courts will order an evaluation of competence once the issue has been raised. Commenting on its decision in *Pate,* the U.S. Supreme Court in *Drope v. Missouri* (1975) noted that,

> evidence of a defendant's irrational behavior, his demeanor at trial, and any prior medical opinion on competence to stand trial are all relevant in determining whether further inquiry is required, but that even one of these factors standing alone may, in some circumstances, be sufficient. (p. 180)

[A] The reader is referred to pp. 20 – 26 of the Brief for the American Psychiatric Association and American Academy of Psychiatry and the Law as *amici curiae* in support of neither party for further elaboration on the expanded abilities required for self-representation.

The *Drope* decision added that, even when a defendant is competent at the outset of trial, the trial court should be aware of any changes in a defendant's condition that might raise question about his competence to stand trial. Thus, the issue of competency can be raised at any time prior to or during a trial.

Evaluating Competency

EVALUATORS

It has long been established that medical professionals may offer an opinion on the issue of competency; however, the role of psychologists in evaluating competency was established in 1962, in *Jenkins v. United States*. The trial judge in *Jenkins* had instructed the jury to disregard the testimony of three psychologists because they were not qualified to diagnose mental disorder. Although *Jenkins* was a case involving an insanity defense, the U.S. Supreme Court's decision to reject the trial judge's opinion established the qualifications of psychologists to provide expert opinion regarding mental disorders. It is important to recognize, however, that this decision does not automatically grant psychologists expert status. Rather, it explicitly stated that the determination of a psychologist's status must be based on the psychologist's nature and extent of knowledge. In the context of competency evaluations, we agree explicitly with this perspective and note that a degree in psychology does not necessarily establish expertise in the evaluation of CST.

Virtually all states now allow testimony by psychologists in competency as well as criminal responsibility issues (Farkas, DeLeon, & Newman,

1997). More recently, psychologists in Canada have gained credibility as experts in competency cases (see Viljoen, Roesch, Ogloff, & Zapf, 2003, for a review).

SETTING

A competency evaluation can take place in a number of settings, including jails, outpatient settings, or inpatient forensic facilities. The common practice of inpatient evaluation has gradually changed over the past few decades and, at present, an increasing number of evaluations are conducted on an outpatient basis, such as at the jail or in a noncustody setting (Grisso, Cocozza, Steadman, Fisher, & Greer, 1994). As we will discuss in Chapter 3, this shift is supported by cost-effectiveness arguments as well as the fact that the majority of decisions about competence can be made in a relatively brief period of time.

One reason that decisions about the competence of most defendants can be made in a brief evaluation is that the threshold for ordering a competency evaluation is low. Evaluators should be aware of the possibility that competency evaluations may occasionally be used for reasons other than concern about a defendant's actual competency. Alternative reasons include delaying a trial, obtaining information that can be useful to the defense, obtaining information about the feasibility of mounting an insanity defense, or other strategic reasons (Cooper & Grisso, 1997; Roesch & Golding, 1980). Changes in *civil commitment* practices that began with the deinstitutionalization movement may also account for the increase in competency referrals over the past several decades. Individuals who previously might have been civilly committed, but who currently do not meet the more stringent dangerousness criteria, may be arrested, and competency referrals become a mechanism to get them into a treatment facility (Melton et al., 2007; Roesch & Golding, 1985).

Often, assessments of competency, especially screening evaluations at the jail or at the court, may take place in less-than-optimal evaluation environments, with multiple distractions. As will be discussed further in Chapter 4, it is important that the evaluation take place in a relatively private, distraction-free setting. When this is not possible, the evaluator may need to request a different setting for the evaluation.

Determination of Competency

Once the evaluation has been completed and a report submitted to the court, a hearing will be scheduled to adjudicate the issue of competence (these hearings usually take place in front of a judge, but a few jurisdictions allow for a jury to hear the issue of competency in certain circumstances). *Cooper v. Oklahoma* (1996) established that incompetency must be proved by a preponderance of evidence, and not the higher standard of clear and convincing evidence. The evaluator's report is highly influential in the court's decisions. Often, the opinion of a clinician is not disputed, and the court may simply accept the recommendations made in the report. Indeed, research has shown that the courts agree with report recommendations upward of 90% of the time (Hart & Hare, 1992; Reich & Tookey, 1986; Roesch & Golding, 1980; Zapf, Hubbard, Cooper, Wheeles, & Ronan, 2004). Thus, this appears to be the norm in those jurisdictions in which the court orders only one evaluator to assess competency. Hearings on the issue of competency appear to occur more often, although still relatively infrequently, in those jurisdictions where two experts are asked to evaluate competency.

Defendants determined to be competent may then proceed with trial or with another disposition of their criminal case. The trial of defendants found incompetent is postponed until competency has been restored or, in a small percentage of cases, until a determination is made that the defendant is unlikely to regain competency. In the next section, we will review legal cases regarding the treatment of incompetent defendants.

Competence Restoration
DETENTION
Until the landmark case of *Jackson v. Indiana* (1972), most states allowed the automatic and indefinite confinement of incompetent defendants. This resulted in many defendants being held for lengthy periods of time, often beyond the sentence that might have been imposed had they been convicted. Roesch and Golding (1980)

CASE LAW

Jackson v. Indiana (1972)

● U.S. Supreme Court held that incompetent defendants could not be confined for more than a reasonable period of time needed to determine if they were capable of regaining capacity in the future.

found, for example, that incompetent defendants in North Carolina were held for an average of nearly three years, with a range up to more than 15 years. This practice was challenged in *Jackson*. The U.S. Supreme Court in *Jackson* held that defendants committed solely on the basis of incompetency "cannot be held more than the reasonable period of time necessary to determine whether there is a substantial probability that he will attain that capacity in the foreseeable future" (p. 738). The Court did not specify limits to the length of time a defendant could reasonably be held, nor did it indicate how progress toward the goal of regaining competency could be assessed. Nevertheless, this decision resulted in changes to state laws regarding confinement of incompetent defendants.

Many states now place limits on the maximum length of time a defendant can be held and, if a defendant is determined to be unlikely to ever regain competency, the commitment based on incompetency must be terminated. However, in many states, the actual impact of *Jackson* may be minimal (Morris, Haroun, & Naimark, 2004). State laws regarding treatment of incompetent defendants vary considerably, and Morris and colleagues found that many states ignore or circumvent *Jackson* by imposing lengthy commitment periods before a determination of unrestorability can be made, or tie the length of confinement to the sentence that could have been imposed had the individual been convicted of the original charge(s). Even after a period of confinement and a determination that competency is unlikely to be restored in the foreseeable future, it is possible that such defendants could be civilly committed, but *United States v. Duhon* (2000) makes clear that defendants who are not dangerous must be released. Charges against defendants who are not restorable are typically dismissed, although sometimes with the provision that they can be reinstated if competency is regained.

MEDICATION

As we will review in Chapter 3, medication is the most common form of treatment for incompetent defendants and, in many cases, for allowing defendants to proceed with trial. Defendants who have been found incompetent but who respond to medication may be returned to court, and a hearing may determine that they are now trial competent. Clinicians should be clear in reports to the court about the role that medication plays in maintaining competency. Since trial is often delayed for some period after a determination of competency is made, it is possible that some defendants will discontinue medication before or even during a trial. If a defendant's behavior changes, it is possible that another competency hearing may be necessary. For example in *Miles v. Stainer* (1997), an Appeals Court held that the trial court had erred when it did not determine whether a defendant had been taking his medication prior to accepting a plea. In this case, the treating physician had been clear that the defendant's competency depended on continuing to take antipsychotic medication, and jail records indicated that the defendant had stopped taking his medication two weeks prior to the plea.

Incompetent defendants may refuse to take medication. In these cases, is it permissible to override their right to refuse treatment and subject them to involuntary medication? Two major cases have been decided by the U.S. Supreme Court, dealing with the issue of the involuntary medication of defendants who had been found IST. In *Riggins v. Nevada* (1992), David Riggins had been prescribed thioridazine (Mellaril®) and found CST. He submitted a motion requesting that he be allowed to discontinue the use of this medication during trial, to show jurors his true mental state at the time of the offense, since he was raising an insanity defense. His motion was denied, and he was convicted of murder and sentenced to death. The U.S. Supreme Court reversed his conviction, holding that his rights were violated. Specifically, the Court found that the trial court failed to establish the need for and medical appropriateness of the medication. The Court commented that "Due process certainly would have been satisfied had the State shown that the treatment was medically appropriate and, considering less intrusive

CASE LAW

Riggins v.
Nevada (1992)

● Permitted the use of involuntary medication if it is established that the treatment is medically appropriate and that any side effects will not undermine the fairness of a trial

alternatives, essential for Riggins' own safety or the safety of others" (p. 127). The Court also addressed the issue of whether the involuntary use of antipsychotic medications may affect the trial's outcome: "Mellaril's side effects may have impacted not only his outward appearance, but also his testimony's content, his ability to follow the proceedings, or the substance of his communication with counsel" (p. 127).

In the case of *Sell v. United States* (2003), the U.S. Supreme Court further specified the criteria to be followed to determine if forced medication is permissible. Dr. Charles Sell, a dentist who had a long history of mental illness, was charged with fraud and attempted murder. Although initially found competent and released on bail, his condition deteriorated and his bail was subsequently revoked. He was reevaluated, found incompetent, and committed for treatment at a Federal Medical Center. Dr. Sell refused to consent to treatment, and the center ordered his involuntary medication. Sell appealed, but the appellate court authorized forced administration of antipsychotic drugs. The appellate court held that Sell was dangerous to himself or others and that medication was necessary to render him less dangerous, that the drug's benefits outweighed the risks, and that the drugs were substantially likely to restore competence. The U.S. Supreme Court held that antipsychotic drugs could be administered against the defendant's will for the purpose of restoring competency, but only in limited circumstances. Writing for the majority, Justice Breyer noted that involuntary medication of incompetent defendants should be rare, and identified several factors that a court must consider in determining whether a defendant can be forced to take medication:

> First, a court must find that *important* governmental interests are at stake. The Government's interest in bringing to trial an individual accused of a serious crime is important. However,

courts must consider each case's facts in evaluating this interest because special circumstances may lessen its importance, e.g., a defendant's refusal to take drugs may mean lengthy confinement in an institution, which would diminish the risks of freeing without punishment one who has committed a serious crime. In addition to its substantial interest in timely prosecution, the Government has a concomitant interest in assuring a defendant a fair trial. . . .

Second, the court must conclude that forced medication will *significantly further* those concomitant state interests. It must find that medication is substantially likely to render the defendant competent to stand trial and substantially unlikely to have side effects that will interfere significantly with the defendant's ability to assist counsel in conducting a defense. . . .

Third, the court must conclude that involuntary medication is *necessary* to further those interests and find that alternative, less intrusive treatments are unlikely to achieve substantially the same results. . . .

Fourth, the court must conclude that administering the drugs is *medically appropriate*. The specific kinds of drugs at issue may matter here as elsewhere. Different kinds of antipsychotic drugs may produce different side effects and enjoy different levels of success. (p. 167, italics in original)

Although the U.S. Supreme Court affirmed that it is permissible to administer antipsychotic drugs to a criminal defendant in order to restore competency, it held that the lower court in Sell's case did not determine that all the above criteria had been met. Consequently, the order to involuntary administer medication was reversed. The Court noted that the government could pursue the request for involuntary medication on the grounds discussed in its decision in *Sell*.

Forensic Mental Health Concepts | 2

E valuation of a defendant's psychological functioning is an essential component of the assessment of competency. Although not clearly specified in the *Dusky* decision (see Chapter 1), most state laws require that a finding of incompetence be based on the presence of a mental disorder (Zapf, 2002). Once the presence of mental disease or defect has been established, the following must ensue:

- evaluation of relevant functional abilities and deficits,
- determination of a causal connection between any noted deficits and mental disorder, and
- specification of how these deficits may impact upon functioning at trial.

In this chapter, we will provide an overview of mental health concepts and present a framework for assessing competence based on a functional, contextual perspective.

Mental Illness as a Prerequisite for Incompetence

Forensic evaluators should recognize that determination of a serious mental disorder or mental retardation is merely the first step in finding a defendant Incompetent to Stand Trial (IST). As Zapf, Skeem, and Golding (2005) noted, "the presence of cognitive disability or mental disorder is merely a threshold issue that must be established to 'get one's foot in the competency door'" (p. 433). Although evaluators a few decades ago appeared to base competency decisions largely on a finding of psychosis or mental retardation (see Roesch & Golding,

INFO

The presence of a mental disorder in itself does not make a defendant incompetent. Rather, a connection must exist between the defendant's specific symptoms and functioning during legal proceedings.

1980, for a review), evaluators now recognize that the presence of a diagnosis, even of a severe mental disorder, is not by itself sufficient to find a defendant incompetent. As detailed in Chapter 3, psychosis is significantly correlated with a finding of incompetence. That is, a majority of incompetent defendants are diagnosed with some form of psychosis (mental retardation and organic brain disorders account for most of the remaining diagnoses). However, only about one-half of evaluated defendants with psychosis are found incompetent (Nicholson & Kugler, 1991), a clear indication that evaluators do not equate incompetence with psychosis. Rather, as discussed later in this chapter, it is necessary to delineate a clear link (causal connection) between a defendant's mental impairments and his ability to participate in legal proceedings. This is referred to as a *functional assessment of competency.*

Before turning to a discussion of functional assessment, it may be helpful to provide a brief overview of mental disorders and their possible relevance to an assessment of CST. A defendant may have clearly demonstrable pathology, but the symptoms or observable features may be irrelevant to the issue of competency. Such features would include depersonalization, derealization, suicidal ideation, and poor insight. Even a person who meets civil commitment criteria may be considered CST, although there does appear to be a strong relationship between incompetence and commitability. For the most part, evaluators need to determine that the level of mental disorder is severe enough to affect a defendant's ability to proceed with trial. A diagnosis is useful in this regard, but evaluators will want to pay more attention to symptoms rather than to broad diagnostic categories. Many incompetent defendants have a diagnosis of schizophrenia, for example, but it is the specific symptoms that will be relevant to the competency evaluation.

Psychiatric Diagnoses and Symptoms

The *Diagnostic and Statistical Manual of Mental Disorders, Fourth Edition, Text Revision* (*DSM-IV-TR*; American Psychiatric Association, 2000) is the standard diagnostic reference used by mental health professionals in North America. No particular diagnosis would rule out a finding of incompetence, but psychotic disorders—along with mental retardation and organic disorders—are those that are more frequently associated with IST. Schizophrenia is a common diagnosis among incompetent defendants largely because it includes psychotic symptoms as the prominent aspect of the diagnosis (Hart & Hare, 1992; Warren, Fitch, Dietz, & Rosenfeld, 1991). As the *DSM-IV-TR* notes, "the term *psychotic* refers to delusions, any prominent hallucinations, disorganized speech, or disorganized or catatonic behavior" (p. 297). These symptoms have been found to be among the strongest predictors of an incompetency determination (Nicholson & Kugler, 1991). Rosenfeld and Wall (1998) found that thought disorder, delusions, paranoia, disorientation, and hallucinations were the best predictors of incompetence among defendants with a diagnosis of psychosis. One of their findings may be particularly instructive for clinicians conducting competency evaluations. They noted that higher levels of psychotic symptoms were associated with impaired ability to assist in one's defense, but disorientation and overall intellectual functioning were associated with impaired ability to understand charges and proceedings. Viljoen, Roesch, and Zapf (2002b) found that defendants with primary psychotic disorders demonstrated more impairment than did other defendants in their understanding of interrogation rights, the nature and object of the proceedings, the possible consequences of proceedings, and their ability to communicate with counsel; however, psychosis was of limited value as a predictor, as high rates of legal impairment were found even in defendants with no diagnosed major mental illness. These studies reinforce the need to focus on the relationship of symptoms (and not broad diagnostic categories or the presence or absence of psychosis) to specific legal abilities.

In Chapter 5, evaluation procedures for assessing mental status are reviewed in detail. Whatever clinical assessment

INFO

Psychotic symptoms are among the strongest predictors of incompetence.

process is used, the following sections delineate crucial elements that need to be assessed and/or ruled out (see Roesch, Zapf, & Eaves, 2006).

FORMAL THOUGHT DISORDER

Gross formal thought disorder or disorganized thinking is an important feature of schizophrenia. It is indicated by disorganized speech (e.g., loose associations, tangentiality, incoherence, or word salad) and is often accompanied by other psychotic features. Disorganized thinking can interfere with the ability to give coherent, relevant instructions to a defense attorney, the capacity to provide testimony at trial, or to understand what witnesses are saying. Motor or sensory aphasia may also need to be considered because of their impact on the ability to communicate.

CONCENTRATION DEFICITS

Concentration deficits may result from severe anxiety, hypomania, mania, organic brain dysfunction, severe attention deficit disorder, or other mental impairment. If severe, these deficits might interfere with the defendant's ability to follow the court process and to instruct counsel as the case unfolds.

RATE OF THINKING

Abrupt and rapid changes in speech (e.g., flight of ideas) can indicate manic behavior and disorganization that would affect a defendant's ability to focus attention on her case. Conversely, profound slowing (retardation) of thinking associated with depression can have the same effect.

DELUSIONS OR HALLUCINATIONS

Delusions and hallucinations are two primary symptoms of psychosis and are particularly relevant to a defendant's CST. As discussed in this chapter, however, it is not simply the presence or absence of delusions that is relevant, but rather the impact of the degree of intrusiveness of abnormal ideation or perception on the defendant's ability to proceed with trial (see Goldstein & Burd, 1990). To be considered incompetent, false ideas or hallucinatory experiences must interfere, at least to some extent, with the ability to think clearly and logically in areas relevant to CST. Gross delusions may not necessarily inhibit the ability to instruct counsel if the subject of the delusions is irrelevant to the defendant's situation or if the delusions are not generally intrusive. However, a delusion causing a defendant to be suspicious of counsel or of the court process itself might impair her ability to give appropriate instructions. For example, Goldstein and Burd cite the case of a 27-year-old man with religious delusions who believed that women were inferior and, consequently, he could not be adequately represented by his female lawyer; however, he also believed that God knew that the complainant was lying and would take her firstborn child, adding that he did not care what happened to him as "only God knows and judges" (p. 380). The concern about representation could be addressed by assigning a male lawyer, but the delusions about God being the sole judge of his guilt or innocence affected his ability to participate in trial strategy. As such, he was found IST.

MEMORY DEFICITS

Memory for the circumstances surrounding the alleged offense would appear to be a critical component of competent participation in the legal process. To prepare a defense, lawyers need to know the circumstances surrounding the arrest of their client, what was said to arresting officers, or information about alibis. What happens in a case in which a defendant cannot remember the arrest or the period immediately preceding the arrest? Interestingly, the courts have not been receptive to the notion that a defendant with amnesia is necessarily incapable of standing trial. As discussed in Chapter 1, the case of *Wilson v. United States* (1968) made clear that amnesia could be a factor, but it must be shown that the amnesia affected the defendant's ability to consult with and assist his lawyer, or affected the defendant's ability to testify in his own behalf. We will return to a discussion of the *Wilson* case later in this chapter when we consider aspects of a functional assessment.

MENTAL RETARDATION (INTELLECTUAL AND DEVELOPMENTAL DISABILITIES)

Another diagnostic category that may be relevant in a competency evaluation is mental retardation, now commonly referred to as intellectual and developmental disability. Mild mental retardation may not impair a person's ability to instruct counsel, but severe intellectual deficits, whether inherited or acquired, may have an adverse effect on the defendant's ability to communicate with counsel or even to understand the nature and purpose of the proceeding (see *United States v. Duhon*, 2000; also, Appelbaum, 1994). A defendant's intellectual capacity may limit her ability to understand the charges and/or the legal procedures, and may also affect her ability to make important case decisions, such as whether to agree to a plea bargain or to testify. Thus, mental retardation is a possible basis for a finding of IST.

Research that has examined the rates of incompetence of individuals with mental retardation has found wide variation. Roesch and Golding (1980) found that 18% of all incompetent defendants in their North Carolina sample were diagnosed with mental retardation, whereas 6% of the competent sample had this diagnosis. Other studies have reported rates ranging from 12% to 36% (Cochrane, Grisso, & Frederick, 2001; Petrella, 1992). Everington and Dunn (1995) found that 57% of mentally retarded defendants evaluated in Ohio were considered IST.

Again, it is important for evaluators to bear in mind that lower intellectual functioning is not, by itself, a basis for a finding of incompetence; it must also be shown how the impairment affects the defendant's capacity to function in the legal context.

INFO

Intellectual impairment may or may not lead to a finding of IST. The impairment must be related to an inability to function in the legal context.

Defendants with intellectual impairments may often be over-looked by defense attorneys and the courts as a group at risk for being IST (Bonnie, 1992a). In their New York state sample of 188 cases, Rosenfeld and Wall (1998) found that only two defendants with mental retardation were referred for a competency evaluation, and both were found to be competent. These authors believed that this does not reflect the actual numbers of cognitively impaired defendants in New York, and they suggested that many such defendants accept plea bargains or proceed to trial without an evaluation of their competency to do so. Bonnie also believed this to be the case, as many individuals with mental retardation are compliant and cooperative with authority figures, such as judges or lawyers, and may pretend to understand their lawyers when, in fact, they may not. He added, however, that empirical data to document this is not available.

Obviously, if intellectual capacity appears to be an issue, evaluators will want to administer intelligence and other psychological tests in addition to competency instruments (see Schlesinger, 2003, for a review). As noted in Chapter 3, instruments designed specifically for assessing legal abilities in possibly intellectually challenged defendants (such as the *Competence Assessment for Standing Trial for Defendants with Mental Retardation* [CAST*MR; Everington & Luckasson, 1992]) may prove particularly useful. As with any forensic assessment, evaluators should be cognizant of the possibility that defendants may be feigning deficits. Everington, Notario-Small, and Horton (2007) found that defendants with mental retardation could understand an instruction to feign their performance on the CAST*MR.

Psycholegal Abilities

A review of competency case law (including *Dusky, Drope, Wieter, Godinez,* and other relevant cases), legal commentary (such as Bonnie's reconceptualization of the construct of competence, discussed next), and the available body of literature on competency evaluation and research indicates a number of psycholegal abilities relevant to the issue of competence.

Conceptualization of the *Dusky* Standard

In 1960, the U.S. Supreme Court articulated the *Dusky* standard in a single sentence. Since that time, research and commentary on the conceptualization of competence have attempted to deconstruct the *Dusky* standard into meaningful prongs with practical operationalization for forensic evaluators. Rogers (2001) described three different conceptualizations of the *Dusky* standard: the three-prong discrete abilities model, the two-prong syntactical analysis model, and the two-prong cognitive complexity model.

The three-prong discrete abilities model operationalizes each component of *Dusky*: rational ability to consult, factual understanding of the courtroom proceedings, and rational understanding of the courtroom proceedings. The two-prong syntactical analysis model breaks *Dusky* into two components on the basis of sentence structure: rational ability to consult, and factual and rational understanding of the proceedings. The two-prong cognitive complexity model breaks *Dusky* into two components on the basis of cognitive abilities: factual understanding and rational abilities.

Bonnie's Reconceptualization of Competence

Bonnie (1992b, 1993) provided a theoretical reformulation of the construct of competence to stand trial, reframed as *adjudicative competence*. Bonnie proposed that criminal competence (adjudicative competence) be conceptualized in terms of two separate but related constructs—a foundational construct (competence to assist counsel) and a contextualized construct (decisional competence)—and argued that the tests of decisional competence should vary according to context.

According to Bonnie (1992b), the foundational construct of competence to assist counsel refers to "the minimum conditions required for participating in one's own defense" (p. 297). He indicated that most U.S. courts have agreed that this includes the individual's

> (i) capacity to understand the charges, the purpose of the criminal process and the adversary system, especially the role of the defense counsel; (ii) capacity to appreciate one's situation as a defendant in

INFO

Bonnie's conceptualization of adjudicative competence is a two-construct model:

- Foundational construct: competence to assist counsel

- Contextualized construct: decisional competence

the criminal prosecution; and (iii) ability to recognize and relate pertinent information to counsel concerning the facts of the case. (p. 297)

If a defendant were to possess these abilities, Bonnie argued, the dignity and reliability of the criminal process would be preserved. This foundational construct of competence to assist counsel does not encompass the defendant's ability to make decisions or the defendant's behavioral functioning at the trial. These abilities, Bonnie asserted, are part of the construct of decisional competence.

Decisional competence, according to Bonnie, is conceptually and clinically distinct from competence to assist counsel. He noted that "although the relevant psychological capacities may overlap, decision-making about defense strategy encompasses conceptual abilities, cognitive skills, and capacities for rational thinking that are not required for assisting counsel" (p. 305). The tests of decisional competence, therefore, should be contextualized (i.e., tailored to the specific situation and the decision that is required).

BONNIE'S TWO-STEP APPROACH TO ADJUDICATIVE COMPETENCE

Bonnie formulated a two-construct model and, therefore, a two-step approach to adjudicative competence. He argued that all defendants must possess the abilities encompassed in the foundational construct of competence to assist counsel. If a defendant lacks any of these abilities, then she should not be allowed to proceed. He argued that this would satisfy the need for dignity and reliability in the criminal process. Bonnie proposed that the bar against adjudication is only absolutely necessary in those cases in which the defendant is incompetent to assist counsel. A defendant's decisional competence, on the other hand, would be evaluated in a context-specific manner, and more flexible responses should be available to deal with deficiencies in a defendant's decisional competence. Although acknowledging that there are certain decisions that counsel could not make (such as waiving certain constitutional rights), Bonnie proposed that surrogate decision making, wherein counsel would make decisions on behalf of the defendant, be used in those cases in which a defendant's decisional competence is questionable. Additionally, stricter tests of decisional competence should be required when the consequences of the decision are great or when the defendant is in disagreement with counsel (i.e., rejecting the advice of counsel).

Bonnie concluded that the use of a two-construct approach to adjudicative competence is compatible with the contemporary understanding of legal incompetence as being contextually bound. In addition, he argued that this two-step approach would remove the necessity that currently exists for legal proceedings to be barred for those found decisionally incompetent. Decisional incompetence could be dealt with through more flexible means, thus allowing some individuals with questionable decisional competence to proceed.

Bonnie's reformulation opened the possibility that defendants could proceed with adjudication, even though, under a single construct approach, they might be considered incompetent. This possibility is illustrated in two cases he presents:

> Suppose a defendant's auditory hallucinations and attentional deficits make it impossible for him to sustain his attention in a courtroom for more than a few minutes. Assume further, however, that his understanding of the charges and the criminal process are unimpaired, he is able to provide pertinent information to his attorney regarding the evidence in the case, and he is able to understand the relevant considerations in deciding whether to accept a proffered plea agreement. In this case, it

might be said that the defendant is competent to plead guilty even though he might not be able to stand trial. In a contrasting case, suppose a defendant is able to communicate rationally with counsel, to pay attention in court, and to understand the nature and purpose of a criminal prosecution and the roles of all the participants. In this case, however, suppose that the defendant is unable, due to mental retardation, to understand the differences between greater- and lesser-included charges, and is unable to understand the probability assessments that are relevant to deciding whether to accept a plea agreement or, if the case is tried, to have a bench trial instead of a jury trial. In this case, it might be said that the defendant is competent to stand trial, but not competent to plead guilty or waive a jury trial. (Bonnie, 1992b, pp. 293–294)

Given the U.S. Supreme Court's opinion in *Godinez* (discussed in Chapter 1), it appears that Bonnie's conceptualization of decisional abilities as being separate and distinct from foundational abilities may be moot. That is, it appears that decisional abilities may be considered part of the competency standard and should be assessed as part of any competency evaluation.

Competence-Relevant Abilities

Bonnie's reconceptualization of competency and the various conceptualizations of *Dusky* and the competency standard reinforce that there are different ways to think about the construct of competence. However, these different conceptualizations hold in common a number of competence-related abilities that should be considered in any competency evaluation.

UNDERSTANDING
"Understanding" generally refers to a defendant's factual understanding and encompasses generalized knowledge that does not involve memory of a specific

INFO

Relevant psycholegal abilities include

● understanding,

● appreciation,

● reasoning,

● consulting with counsel,

● assisting in one's defense, and

● decision-making abilities.

event and the ability to recall overlearned material (semantic memory). Within the context of CST, factual understanding generally encompasses the ability to comprehend general information about the arrest process and courtroom proceedings including

- the roles of key participants within the legal process (e.g., defense counsel, prosecutor, judge, jury, etc.),
- the current charges faced by the defendant,
- the elements of an offense,
- the consequences of conviction (in a general manner), and
- the rights waived in making a guilty plea.

The defendant's factual understanding of the legal process includes a basic knowledge of legal strategies and options, although not necessarily as applied to the defendant's own particular case (case-specific understanding usually is encompassed by appreciation [rational understanding]; see next section). Thus, the competence-related ability to understand involves the defendant's ability to factually understand general, legally relevant information.

APPRECIATION

"Appreciation" generally refers to a defendant's rational understanding and encompasses specific knowledge regarding an accurate perception of information relevant to the role of the defendant in his own case (episodic memory). Within the context of CST, appreciation encompasses the ability to comprehend and accurately perceive specific information regarding how the arrest and courtroom processes have affected or will affect the defendant, including

- the likelihood that she will be found guilty,
- the consequences for the defendant of being convicted (range and nature of possible penalties and how they will affect the defendant),
- the defendant's appraisal of the available legal defenses and their likely outcomes,

- the defendant's appraisal of whether or not to testify, and

- the defendant's ability to make rational decisions regarding the specific case.

The defendant's appraisal of the situation must be reality-based, and any decisions that she makes about the case must be made on the basis of reality-based information. Thus, the competence-related ability to appreciate involves the application of information that the defendant factually understands to the specific case in a rational (i.e., reality-based) manner.

REASONING

"Reasoning" generally refers to a defendant's ability to consider and weigh relevant pieces of information in a rational manner in arriving at a decision or a conclusion. Within the context of CST, reasoning encompasses the ability

- to distinguish more relevant from less relevant information,

- to seek relevant information,

- to weigh and evaluate various legal options and their consequences,

- to make comparisons, and

- to provide reality-based justification for making particular case-specific decisions or conclusions.

To demonstrate appropriate reasoning ability, the defendant must be able to communicate in a coherent manner and make decisions in a rational, reality-based manner undistorted by pathology. It is important to distinguish between the outcome of a decision and the process by which the decision is made. What is important is that the defendant be able to use appropriate reasoning processes—weighing, comparing, and evaluating information—in a rational manner, not the outcome of the decision. In the case of a defendant who is proceeding with the assistance of an attorney, reasoning encompasses the ability of the defendant to consult with counsel and to make rational decisions regarding various aspects of participation in his defense.

ASSISTING COUNSEL

Although the *Dusky* standard indicates that the defendant must be able to "consult with his lawyer," the U.S. Supreme Court in *Drope v. Missouri* (1974) used the terminology "assist in preparing his defense" and the Federal standard (U.S. Code Annotated, Title 18, Part III, chapter 13, section 4241) indicates that the defendant must be able to "assist properly in his defense." Thus, it appears that the defendant's ability to consult with and assist counsel must be considered as part of the competency assessment. Within the context of CST, the ability to assist counsel generally incorporates the defendant's ability to

- consult with counsel,
- relate to the lawyer,
- plan legal strategy,
- engage in her defense,
- challenge witnesses,
- testify relevantly, and
- manage her courtroom behavior.

The defendant must be able to engage with counsel in a rational manner; thus, effectively assisting counsel requires that the defendant be able to communicate coherently and reason (see earlier discussion under Reasoning).

DECISION MAKING

Closely tied to the abilities to appreciate, reason, and assist counsel is the ability to make decisions. The U.S. Supreme Court decision in *Cooper v. Oklahoma* (1996) appeared to equate a defendant's inability to communicate with counsel with incapacity to make fundamental decisions. In addition, the U.S. Supreme Court in *Godinez* incorporated decision-making abilities about the case into the standard for competence. Thus, it appears that a defendant's decision-making abilities with respect to specific, relevant aspects of the case need be considered in the trial competency evaluation.

Although decision-making abilities are incorporated within the competence-related abilities just discussed (appreciation, reasoning, and assisting counsel), the importance of evaluating the defendant's context-specific decision-making abilities warrants highlighting. Research examining the specific competence-related abilities addressed by evaluators in their reports indicates cause for concern with respect to decision making. LaFortune and Nicholson (1995) examined competency evaluation reports and found that of seven competence-related abilities, only the defendant's understanding of the charge was described in the majority of reports. Contextually relevant decisional abilities, such as appreciation of the plea bargaining process, were rarely addressed. Skeem and her colleagues examined competency evaluation reports and also found that certain abilities important and relevant to CST, such as decision-making abilities, were rarely addressed by evaluators in their reports (Skeem, Golding, Cohn, & Berge, 1998). Thus, evaluators should be careful not only to evaluate a defendant's decisional abilities within the context of those decisions that she might reasonably be expected to make during the course of the proceedings, but should also be careful to include this information in their reports.

Functional and Contextual Nature of the Evaluation

Grisso (2003) provided a framework for the assessment of any legal competence. His model begins with a focus on an individual's functional abilities, behaviors, or capacities. He defines functional abilities as "that which an individual can do or accomplish, as well as . . . the knowledge, understanding, or beliefs that may be necessary for the accomplishment" (pp. 23–24).

A functional assessment dictates that CST cannot simply be assessed in the abstract, independent of contextual factors, particularly for those cases in which a finding of incompetence is possible. If a defendant does not have a mental disorder or intellectual deficit, the demands of the defendant's particular legal situation may not be relevant. This is because defendants without a mental disorder or intellectual incapacity will not be found incompetent, so it is not necessary to evaluate case-specific issues. For defendants who do meet the mental status prerequisite, an evaluation of contextual factors should always take place. This is the essence of a functional approach to assessing competence, which posits that the abilities required by the defendant in her specific case should be taken into account when assessing competence. The open-textured, context-dependent nature of the construct of CST was summarized by Golding and Roesch (1988):

> Mere presence of severe disturbance (a psychopathological criterion) is only a threshold issue—it must be further demonstrated that such severe disturbance in *this* defendant, facing *these* charges, *in light of existing* evidence, anticipating the substantial effort of a *particular* attorney with a *relationship of known characteristics,* results in the defendant being unable to rationally assist the attorney or to comprehend the nature of the proceedings and their likely outcome. (p. 79, italics in original)

The importance of a person–context interaction has been highlighted by Grisso (2003). He defined a functional assessment in the following manner:

> A decision about legal competence is in part a statement about *congruency or incongruency between (a) the extent of a person's functional ability and (b) the degree of performance demand that is made* by *the specific instance of the context in that case.* Thus an interaction between individual ability and situational demand, not an absolute level of ability, is of special significance for competence decisions. (pp. 32–33, italics in original)

Skeem and Golding (1998) suggest a three-step procedure for establishing a link between psychopathology and impairment of legal abilities:

> One might (a) carefully consider the nature and content of the defendant's primary symptoms, (b) consider how these symptoms might relate conceptually to the defendant's specific psycholegal impairments, then (c) assess, as directly as possible, whether there actually is a relationship between the symptom and the CST impairment. (p. 364)

Obviously, a functional assessment requires evaluators to learn about what may be required of a particular defendant. Some of this information may be provided by the defendant, but other information will need to come from court documents and from the defendant's attorney. Some cases are more complex than others and may, as a result, require different types of psycholegal abilities. As Rogers and Mitchell (1991) note, the requisite level of understanding for a complex crime is higher than for a less complex one. Thus, it may be that the same defendant is competent for one type of legal proceeding but not for others. In cases in which a trial is likely, a defendant's demeanor in court and the ability to testify will certainly be of relevance. A defendant who is likely to withdraw into a catatonic-like state if required to testify, or one who may appear to jurors as not caring or not paying attention to the trial because of medication side effects, may not be capable of proceeding. But these same defendants may be able to proceed if the attorney intends to plea bargain (the way in which the vast majority of all criminal cases are handled).

The functional approach (see Figure 2.1) is supported by research and scholarly arguments that conclude that competencies in one area of functioning are not necessarily indicative of competencies in other areas (Bonnie, 1992b; Golding & Roesch, 1988; Grisso, Appelbaum, Mulvey, & Fletcher, 1995). In addition, *Wilson v. United States* (1968) is of direct relevance to our discussion of a

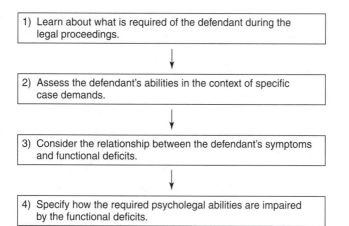

Figure 2.1 Functional Approach

INFO

Utah's (1994) statute provides a model for a functional assessment. It specifies that evaluators must consider a comprehensive range of psycholegal abilities (including the iatrogenic effects of medication and decisional competencies) and also requires judges to identify which psycholegal abilities are impaired when a defendant is found incompetent.

functional assessment. As discussed earlier in this chapter, *Wilson* clearly calls for evaluators to assess the relevance of clinical issues within the context of a particular case. *Wilson* dealt with a case of amnesia, and the holding was such that amnesia *per se* does not constitute incompetence, but we believe the implications of this case are considerably broader. *Wilson* requires an evaluation of many other questions in order to determine whether a defendant's possible deficit could be considered a basis for a finding of incompetence. Can the defense reconstruct the case without input from the defendant? Did the defendant have an alibi (*Wilson* noted that "If there is any substantial possibility that the accused could, but for his amnesia, establish an alibi or other defense, it should be presumed that he would have been able to do so")? How strong is the prosecution's case (*Wilson*, p. 464, noted that "Most important here will be whether the Government's case is such as to negate all reasonable hypotheses of innocence")? These considerations make it evident that an evaluation of competency, particularly one in which a finding of incompetency is possible, requires evaluators to learn more about the details of the case and to assess the defendant's abilities accordingly.

Current Practice

Unfortunately, evaluators often fail to relate specific abilities and deficits to the particular case (Heilbrun & Collins, 1995). Skeem and colleagues (1998) examined the reports of competency evaluators in Utah and found that evaluators place heavy emphasis on basic foundational competence issues (Bonnie's competence to assist counsel construct), but pay little attention in their reports to decisional competence issues. For example, Skeem and colleagues found that only 12% of the reports examined addressed the defendant's understanding of a guilty plea. In addition, although almost all defendants evaluated for CST were on medication at the time of the assessment, only 18% of reports discussed the impact of medication on a defendant's competency. These researchers also noted that the reports rarely provided a discussion of the link between symptomatology and legal abilities. Skeem and colleagues concluded that the current training of forensic evaluators might be insufficient, and they called for both increased training and examination requirements for examiner certification, as well as ongoing monitoring of competency reports.

Summary

In summary, it seems clear that evaluators should adopt a functional approach to the assessment of competency. In addition, forensic mental health experts should ensure that the written reports of their competency evaluations make clear the relationship between symptoms and functional deficits, as well as delineate the specific ways in which a defendant's deficits may impact upon his functioning during the course of the proceedings. More information regarding the contents of written reports is provided in Chapter 7.

Empirical Foundations and Limits | 3

Prior to 1980, research on CST was limited; however, the past few decades have witnessed a surge in research on this issue. In addition, structured and semi-structured instruments for assessing CST have been developed. This chapter provides a comprehensive but concise overview of research on CST and competency assessment instruments.

Research on Examinee Populations and Competency Issues

This section addresses the research on various aspects of the adjudicative competency process, including raising the issue of competency, the characteristics of competent and incompetent defendants, reliability and validity of the evaluation process, and the disposition of defendants found IST.

Raising the Issue of Competency

Adjudicative competence is perhaps the single most commonly raised clinical forensic issue in the criminal justice system. Poythress, Bonnie, Monahan, Otto, and Hoge (2002) estimate, conservatively, that over 60,000 evaluations are conducted annually, making it a far more common referral question than other issues, such as criminal responsibility.

As noted in Chapter 1, any officer of the court can raise the issue of competency although, in practice, it is most often raised by defense attorneys. This makes sense, of course, since defense lawyers typically have the most invested in ensuring that their clients are capable of assisting them in preparing a defense (as will be discussed later in this chapter; however, concerns about competency may not be the only reason that a defense attorney might request a competency evaluation). Poythress and colleagues (2002) reported a series of studies of defense attorneys in several jurisdictions who responded to questions about their perceptions of the competence of their clients. These researchers found that lawyers had concerns about the competency of their clients in 8–15% of cases; however, competency evaluations were requested in less than half of these cases (in some of those cases for which competency evaluations were not requested, the attorney tried to resolve the concerns through informal means, such as including a family member in the decision-making process). Poythress and colleagues noted that the attorneys indicated that their concerns were based on the functional abilities of the clients, such as communicating facts and decision-making capacity.

Despite these results from attorneys, it has been argued that other reasons may prompt a request for a competency evaluation. In their study of North Carolina lawyers, Roesch and Golding (1980) found that attorneys used competency evaluations to determine whether there might be a basis for an insanity defense or to get information that might be useful in plea bargaining or sentencing. In addition, some attorneys may use the competency evaluation as a means of delaying trial. Melton, Petrila, Poythress, and Slobogin (2007) consider this to be the most objectionable misuse of competency referrals, since it deprives defendants of pretrial release and is used simply for strategic reasons, such as in cases in which community outrage is paramount and the lawyer anticipates that, with the passage of time, community resentment will subside.

It may also be the case that competency referrals may be used as a mechanism to get defendants out of jail and into a mental health facility. Beginning with the deinstitutionalization movement in the 1960s and 1970s, jails have seen an increasing number of inmates with mental health problems (Roesch, 1995). Many jails do not have the mental health services and trained personnel required to address the needs of these inmates, so referral to a forensic hospital may be viewed as a viable alternative. Essentially, this functions as a back door into treatment for individuals who are not considered dangerous or would not otherwise meet civil commitment criteria.

Recent developments in jail mental health screening and services may serve to reduce this misuse of competency referrals in the future (Nicholls, Roesch, Olley, Ogloff, & Hemphill, 2005).

Judges may be aware of the possible misuse of competency evaluations but nevertheless routinely grant motions requesting evaluations, perhaps in large part because of a desire to avoid a basis for postconviction appeal. Roesch and Golding (1980) found that North Carolina judges suspected that defense attorneys either misunderstood the competency laws or were attempting to delay trial, but they nevertheless rarely denied such motions.

Reasons other than a concern about a defendant's competency may at least partially account for the consistent finding that only a small percentage of defendants referred for competency evaluations are found incompetent. Roesch and Golding (1980) reported on 10 studies conducted prior to 1980 and found an average incompetency rate of 30%. They also noted a considerable range of rates, with some jurisdictions finding almost no referred defendants to be incompetent, whereas others reported rates as high as 77%. More recent studies have confirmed a low percentage of incompetent defendants, with average estimates at about 20% of referrals being found incompetent, although again, with considerable variation by jurisdiction (Cochrane, Grisso, & Frederick, 2001; Cooper & Zapf, 2003; Nicholson & Kugler, 1991; Warren, Rosenfeld, Fitch, & Hawk, 1997; Zapf & Roesch, 1998, 2005b).

The many and varied uses and misuses of competency evaluation referrals reinforces the importance that clinicians seek information from attorneys regarding the reasons for referral. Such discussions with the defense attorney would ensure that clinicians do not become "unwitting participants in strategic ploys by one side or the other having noth-ing to do with competency—the

INFO

Possible misuses of competency evaluation referrals by defense attorneys include

● to determine whether there might be a basis for an insanity defense,

● to get information that might be useful in plea bargaining or sentencing,

● to delay trial, and

● to get defendants out of jail and into a mental health facility.

ostensible reason for the referral, and the only issue with which clinicians should be concerned" (Melton et al., 2007, p. 134).

The Characteristics of Referred and Incompetent Defendants

REFERRED DEFENDANTS

Defendants referred for competency evaluations are often marginalized individuals with extensive criminal and mental health histories. Research has indicated that the majority of these defendants tends to be male, single, unemployed, with prior criminal histories, prior contact with mental health services, and past psychiatric hospitalizations (Cooper & Zapf, 2003; Martell, Rosner, & Harmon, 1994; Reich & Wells, 1985; Roesch, Ogloff, Hart, Dempster, Zapf, & Whittemore, 1997; Steadman, 1979; Warren, Fitch, Deitz, & Rosenfeld, 1991; Zapf & Roesch, 1998; Zapf, Roesch, & Viljoen, 2001). These results appear to be consistent across both the United States and Canada. In addition, females are referred for competency evaluations far less frequently than males; however, there do not appear to be any gender differences in the rates of incompetency determinations, performance on competency measures, or rates of psychosis (Poythress et al., 2002; Riley, 1998).

Viljoen and Zapf (2002) compared 80 defendants referred for competency evaluation with 80 defendants not referred and found that referred defendants were significantly more likely to meet diagnostic criteria for a current psychotic disorder, be charged with a violent offense, and to demonstrate impaired legal abilities. In addition, referred defendants were less likely to have had previous criminal charges. Notably, approximately 25% of nonreferred defendants demonstrated impairment on competence-related abilities. In addition, approximately 20% of referred defendants either did not meet criteria for a mental disorder or demonstrated no impairment of competence-related abilities.

INCOMPETENT DEFENDANTS

Given that a finding of incompetency is based on both mental disorder and deficits in functional abilities, it is expected that psychosis or mental retardation (intellectual disability) would be prevalent in samples of incompetent defendants. Roesch and Golding (1980) found that psychosis, mental retardation, or organic brain syndrome were diagnosed in nearly their entire sample of 130 incompetent defendants. Conversely, competent defendants were more likely to be diagnosed with substance abuse disorders. Similar findings were reported by Warren, Fitch, Dietz, and Rosenfeld (1991).

Cooper and Zapf (2003) examined the predictive efficiency of various clinical, criminological, and sociodemographic variables in a sample of 468 criminal defendants referred for competency evaluation and found clinical diagnostic variables and employment status to be the only significant predictors of competency status. Incompetent defendants were significantly more likely to be unemployed and to be diagnosed with either psychotic or nonpsychotic major mental disorders and significantly less likely to be diagnosed with substance abuse disorders or minor mental disorders, such as adjustment disorders or personality disorders.

Viljoen, Roesch, and Zapf (2002b) examined the relationship between diagnosis and competence-related abilities and found that defendants with psychotic disorders were more impaired than other defendants in terms of their abilities to understand the nature and object of the proceedings, to appreciate the possible consequences of the proceedings, and to communicate with counsel. However, high rates of legal impairment were also found in defendants without any diagnosed major mental illness, thus limiting the utility of psychosis as a predictor of incompetence.

Nicholson and Kugler (1991) reviewed 30 studies and concluded that defendants with psychotic disorders were more likely to be incompetent. They found 51% of defendants with a diagnosis of psychosis to be incompetent, compared to only 10% without this diagnosis. The Nicholson and Kugler meta-analysis also serves to emphasize that, although psychosis is associated with a finding of incompetence, an almost equal number of defendants with a diagnosis of psychosis are considered to be competent. While psychotic symptomatology may be relevant, the functional approach that we have outlined in this book requires that psychiatric symptoms (mental illness or cognitive impairment) be the cause of any noted functional deficits related to the specific demands of a defendant's case.

Studies focusing on specific symptoms are useful as indicators of the basis for a finding of incompetence. In a comparison of North Carolina competency evaluation reports for competent and incompetent defendants, Roesch and Golding (1980) found that incompetent defendants were significantly more likely to have delusions, hallucinations, confused and incoherent speech, and uncooperative behavior, but unlikely to have a history of alcohol and drug abuse. Rosenfeld and Wall (1998) found that symptoms, rather than diagnoses, were better predictors of competence. Specific symptoms that they found to be predictive of incompetence included disorientation, hallucinations, delusions, paranoia, and mania. Other research has found that impairment in the ability to stand trial is highly correlated with psychotic symptoms of conceptual disorganization and hallucinations, whereas delusions appear to have a weaker and more isolated influence (Goldstein & Burd, 1990; Hoge, Poythress, Bonnie, Monahan, Eisenberg, & Feucht-Haviar, 1997; James, Duffield, Blizard, & Hamilton, 2001).

Research examining the relationships between symptoms and competence-related abilities shows significant relationships between certain types of symptoms and specific legal abilities. For example, Viljoen, Zapf, and Roesch (2003) found conceptual disorganization and unusual thoughts to be strongly related to impairment in the legal abilities measured by the Fitness Interview Test–Revised (FIT-R; Roesch, Zapf, Eaves, & Webster, 1998; Roesch, Zapf, & Eaves, 2006) and depression and withdrawal to be related to impairment on the understanding and reasoning subsections of the MacArthur Competence Assessment Tool–Criminal Adjudication (MacCAT-CA; Hoge, Bonnie, Poythress, & Monahan, 1999; Poythress et al., 1999), respectively.

Reliability and Validity of the Evaluation Process

Since evaluators are assessing a defendant's present ability to perform a series of relatively clearly defined tasks, it seems reasonable to expect that competency evaluations would be highly reliable.

In fact, this is precisely what the numerous studies on reliability have shown, with agreement about the ultimate opinion regarding competency being reported in the 90% range (Cox & Zapf, 2004; Golding, Roesch, & Schreiber, 1984; Poythress & Stock, 1980; Rosenfeld & Ritchie, 1998). However, a *reliable* system of evaluation is not necessarily a *valid* one. For example, at one time, it was the case that evaluators equated psychosis with incompetency (Roesch & Golding, 1980). Thus, if clinicians agreed that a defendant was psychotic, they would also agree that the defendant was incompetent. As noted in this chapter, although psychosis is highly correlated with incompetency, it is also the case that a large percentage of competent defendants experience psychotic symptoms. The view that psychosis and incompetency are not inextricably entwined has changed as evaluators have become better trained and more research is available to guide decisions.

The problem of evaluating validity is that no gold standard exists for competence against which to compare evaluator decisions/opinions. Relying on court decisions is not particularly helpful, since agreement rates between evaluator recommendations and court determinations have been shown to be well over 90% (Cox & Zapf, 2004; Cruise & Rogers, 1998; Hart & Hare, 1992; Reich & Tookey, 1986; Zapf, Hubbard, Cooper, Wheeles, & Ronan, 2004). How, then, can the issue of construct validity be assessed? Golding and colleagues (1984) suggested the use of a panel of experts, referred to as a "blue-ribbon panel," to serve as an independent criterion. In their study, they asked two experts to make judgments about competency, based on a review of records, reports from hospital evaluators, and evaluations using the Interdisciplinary Fitness Interview (IFI; Golding, Roesch, & Schreiber, 1984). Golding and colleagues found that "for the 17 cases seen by the blue-ribbon panelists, they agreed with the IFI panelists 88% of the time, with the hospital staff 82% of the time, and with the courts 88% of the time," and they concluded that "on the basis of these data, it would be hard to argue for one criterion definition over another" (p. 331).

Another possible means by which to study the issue of construct validity might be to set up a "mock trial" situation at a facility where incompetent defendants are committed for restoration.

BEWARE
No "gold
standard"
exists for competence, and
thus there is no means for
establishing the validity of
evaluations.

Defendants' competence-related abilities and deficits could be directly observed "in action" and in conjunction with the assistance of a defense attorney. In addition, a judge could render a disposition regarding competency status. Although this type of research paradigm has yet to be conducted, this might be one way of coming close to solving the construct validity problem.

The aforementioned study illustrates the methodological problems inherent in studies of competency evaluations, particularly in terms of the lack of a "correct" outcome against which to compare different methods of decision making. We are left with the reality that there can be no hard criterion against which to test the validity of competency evaluations, because we do not have a test of how incompetent defendants would perform in the actual criterion situations. Since incompetent defendants are not allowed to go to trial until competency is restored, there is no test of whether a defendant found IST truly would have been unable to proceed with a trial or other judicial proceedings. Short of the provisional trial that will be discussed in the next section, the ultimate test of validity will never be possible.

The Disposition of Defendants Found Incompetent to Stand Trial

The *Jackson v. Indiana* (1972) decision (see Chapter 1) resulted in substantial changes to the disposition of incompetent defendants. *Jackson* held that incompetent defendants could not be held more than a reasonable period of time necessary to determine whether a substantial probability exists that they will attain the capacity in the foreseeable future. The decision in *Jackson* resulted in changes to state laws, serving to restrict the length of hospitalization. Statute changes varied considerably by state, with some states specifying no time limit, some states imposing a defined limit such as 18 months, and still other states tying the length of hospitalization to the severity of charge. As Roesch and Golding (1980) noted, this latter practice appears to be based more on a rationale of punishment than treatment, despite the

fact that incompetent defendants have
not yet been convicted of any crime.
Commitment of incompetent defendants for restoration is automatic and, in
most cases, is inpatient in nature; however, some state statutes do allow for
outpatient commitment for competence

restoration. The American Bar Association has recommended that
defendants be treated in the least restrictive environment; however, inpatient competence restoration still appears to be the norm.

Empirical research on competence restoration indicates that
most defendants are restorable: Nicholson and McNulty (1992)
reported a restoration rate of 95% after an average of two months;
Nicholson, Barnard, Robbins, and Hankins (1994) reported a rate of
90% after an average of 280 days; Cuneo and Brelje (1984) reported
a restoration rate of 74% within one year; and Carbonell, Heilbrun,
and Friedman (1992) reported a rate of about 62% after three
months. Thus, regardless of the upper time limits on competence
restoration allowed by state statute, it is now the case that most
incompetent defendants are returned to court as competent within
six months (Bennett & Kish, 1990; Nicholson & McNulty, 1992;
Pinals, 2005; Poythress et al., 2002), and the vast majority of incompetent defendants are restored to competency within a year.

PREDICTION OF RESTORABILITY

In 1980, Roesch and Golding speculated that forensic mental
health professionals were limited in their ability to predict which
defendants would not be restorable to competence. Research
since that time has confirmed that the ability of evaluators to predict competence restoration is poor (Carbonnell, Heilbrun, &
Friedman, 1992; Hubbard, Zapf, & Ronan, 2003; Nicholson &
McNulty, 1992; Nicholson et al., 1994). A study by Cuneo and
Brelje (1984) illustrates the problems in predicting restoration.
These researchers found a 78% accuracy rate for professionals
who were asked to predict whether competency would be
restored within one year. Although, at first glance, this rate may
seem impressive, it becomes less so when the high base rate for

restoration is taken into consideration (i.e., the fact that most defendants are restored within a six-month period). The false-positive rate (i.e., proportion of defendants who are predicted to regain competency but do not) is a more appropriate statistic to evaluate the ability to accurately predict responsiveness to treatment. In the Cuneo and Brelje (1984) study, the false-positive rate was 23%. Thus, evaluators appear to have difficulty identifying the smaller percentage of incompetent defendants who will not respond to treatment.

Hubbard and Zapf (2003) used logistic regression to investigate the variables related to predictions of restorability for a sample of 89 incompetent defendants, and found that current violent charge and previous criminal history were the two most significant predictors of restorability decisions. When criminal, diagnostic, and sociodemographic variables were considered individually, defendants predicted not restorable were more likely to be older and to have impairment in the ability to understand information about the legal process, whereas those predicted to be restorable were more likely to have less serious diagnoses (nonpsychotic minor mental disorders) and more serious, violent criminal histories (Hubbard, Zapf, & Ronan, 2003).

A recent Ohio study by Mossman (2007), however, suggests that certain variables may hold promise for predicting nonrestorability. Mossman found that individuals with a long-standing psychotic disorder with lengthy periods of prior psychiatric hospitalizations or irremediable cognitive deficits such as mental retardation were well below average in terms of their chances of restoration.

The growing literature on prediction of restorability has implications for both assessment and treatment. Research identifying the strongest predictors of restorability should be incorporated into the initial assessment of competency, in responding to the issue of probability of restoration for defendants considered incompetent. In addition, this research has implications for intervention planning in that being able to identify those who will be difficult to restore would allow for an earlier start in an intensive restoration track that might serve to reduce the amount of time spent treating incompetent individuals before recommending to the court that they are unable to be restored. Finally, what this literature makes clear is that it is rare that an incompetent individual will not be restored. Thus, it would be inappropriate to conclude, at the initial competency evaluation stage, that an individual who appears incompetent would not be restorable within the foreseeable future.

COMPETENCE RESTORATION TREATMENT

The most common form of treatment for the restoration of competence involves the administration of psychotropic medication. Some jurisdictions have also established educational treatment programs designed to increase a defendant's understanding of the legal process or individualized treatment programs that confront the problems that hinder a defendant's ability to participate in her defense (Bertman et al., 2003; Davis, 1985; Pendleton, 1980; Siegal & Elwork, 1990). In addition, some jurisdictions have implemented treatment programs specifically targeted toward those defendants with mental retardation who are found incompetent to proceed.

Siegal and Elwork (1990) evaluated the use of an educational program as part of the competence restoration process by comparing randomly assigned control and experimental groups wherein the experimental group included the use of a videotape that described the roles of courtroom personnel and court procedure, as well as group problem-solving sessions in which problems arising from a subject's actual legal case were presented and discussed. Results showed greater improvement on competency assessment instrument scores for the experimental group and a greater number of staff recommendations of competence to stand trial (at 45 days after treatment, 43% of the treated group, but only 15% of the controls, were considered competent by staff).

The success of treatment programs for the restoration of competence is variable and depends upon the nature of the

INFO

Competence restoration treatment may include

- psychotropic medication,
- educational programs, and
- individualized treatment.

treatment program and the type of defendant targeted. Anderson and Hewitt (2002) examined treatment programs designed to restore competency in defendants with mental retardation and found that only 18% of their sample was restored. These researchers concluded, "for the most part, competency training for defendants with MR [mental retardation] might not be that effective" (p. 349). Other researchers and commentators have found similar results and have noted the difficulty in treating a chronic condition such as mental retardation (Daniel & Menninger, 1983; Ellis & Luckasson, 1985).

Treatment programs that target defendants with various other types of mental disorders have met with more success in that larger proportions of the defendants are restored to competency; however, it is not clear that individualized treatment programs that target specific underlying deficits for each defendant are any more effective than educational programs that teach defendants about their legal rights (Bertman et al., 2003). What appears to be accurate is that successful restoration is related to how well the defendant responds to psychotropic medications administered to alleviate those symptoms of the mental disorder that initially impaired those functional abilities associated with trial competency.

PROVISIONAL TRIALS

One alternative to treatment, especially when it appears that treatment is likely to be lengthy, is to allow possibly incompetent defendants to proceed with their criminal cases (Burt & Morris, 1972; Roesch & Golding, 1980). This may, at first blush, appear to be contradictory, since competency laws were designed to protect the rights of incompetent defendants to a fair trial. However, as Gobert (1973) commented, the consequences of denying a trial results in the loss of a number of rights: "Effectively lost are his rights to jury trial, to confront witnesses, to call witnesses in his own behalf, to take the stand on his own behalf, and to have his guilt determined beyond a reasonable doubt" (p. 668). Allowing a trial would provide an opportunity to advance a defense to any criminal charges and force the state to show that it had sufficient evidence for a conviction. Roesch and Golding (1980) commented that allowing a trial would serve as a true test of judgments that a defendant is IST, in that clinicians could directly assess a defendant's capacities in

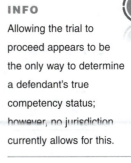

INFO

Allowing the trial to proceed appears to be the only way to determine a defendant's true competency status; however, no jurisdiction currently allows for this.

the actual criterion situation. If a defendant were acquitted, the issue of competency would be moot. If convicted, the verdict could be set aside if evidence was presented that the defendant's competency was an issue.

3
chapter

Competency Assessment Methods

In this section, various competency assessment methods will be reviewed, with a specific focus on the available competency assessment instruments. The reader is referred to additional sources for more detailed information on the various competency assessment instruments discussed (see Grisso, 1986, 2003; Melton, Petrila, Poythress, & Slobogin, 1997; Roesch, Zapf, Golding, & Skeem, 1999; Zapf & Viljoen, 2003).

Clinical Interview

The clinical interview remains to this day the primary method used to evaluate CST. Given the contextual nature of the competency construct and the emphasis on functional abilities, it is impossible to evaluate a defendant's competency without engaging in a clinical interview. Although much commentary exists regarding the unreliability of clinical decision making, no research has examined the reliability of the clinical interview as a competency evaluation method *per se*; however, research has indicated that the use of competency assessment instruments (discussed in the next section) serves to increase the reliability of competency determinations

(Golding, Roesch, & Schreiber, 1984; Nicholson & Kugler, 1991; Skeem, Golding, Cohn, & Berge, 1998).

Forensic Assessment Instruments

In addition to simply using a clinical interview, Grisso (2003) delineated three logical benefits of using *forensic assessment instruments* (FAIs) in the evaluation of competency:

- they provide structure for the examiner,

- they may improve communication in legal settings, and

- they "facilitate empirical research on the associations between legally relevant functional abilities (operationally defined by FAIs) and the constructs of psychiatry and psychology (operationally defined by more traditional, clinical instruments)," which "provides an empirical basis for mental health professionals to employ when interpreting individual cases" (p. 46).

Prior to the 1960s, no FAIs (a term coined by Grisso in 1986) existed to assist experts in the evaluation of various legal issues. Trial competency was the first area for which FAIs were developed. The evolution of FAIs for the evaluation of competency has gone from early checklists (i.e., Robey, 1965; Bukatman, Foy, & de Grazia, 1971) and sentence completion tasks (i.e., Lipsitt, Lelos, & McGarry, 1971) to self-report questionnaires (i.e., Barnard et al., 1991), to interview-based instruments without, and then with, criterion-based scoring. This section provides a brief review of many of the competency assessment instruments, as well as a review of the research conducted using these instruments to assist evaluators in selecting an appropriate instrument to aid in the evaluation of competency. We have used three categories to organize this section: *nomothetic* instruments (those based on generalized, normative interpretation), *idiographic* instruments (those focused on the specific and contextual characteristics of the individual being evaluated), and instruments for use with special populations. Within each section, we move from the more recently developed instruments to the older instruments.

NOMOTHETIC INSTRUMENTS

The Evaluation of Competency to Stand Trial–Revised The ECST-R (Rogers, Tillbrook, & Sewell, 2004) was designed to be congruent with the *Dusky* standard. It is a hybrid interview, containing both semi-structured and structured components, designed to assess CST generally, as well as specific competencies such as competence to plead and competence to proceed *pro se*. The ECST-R takes approximately 30 minutes to administer, and its structure provides a "focus on case-specific information that is relevant to the pending case and the individual's relationship with his or her defense counsel" (Rogers et al., 2004, p. 9). The ECST-R is comprised of 18 items, yielding scores on four different scales:

1. Factual Understanding of the Courtroom Proceedings (FAC; six items),
2. Rational Understanding of the Courtroom Proceedings (RAC; seven items),
3. Consult with Counsel (CWC; six items), and
4. Overall Rational Ability (raw scores for RAC and CWC combined).

In addition, the ECST-R contains 28 items that yield scores on five *response style* scales that screen for feigned incompetency:

1. realistic (nine items),
2. psychotic (nine items),
3. nonpsychotic (nine items),
4. impairment (19 items), and
5. both psychotic and nonpsychotic (18 items).

Each item on the ECST-R is scored on the basis of ratings (which can range from one to several for each item), and scale scores are obtained by summing the raw scores for each relevant item; however,

3
chapter

INFO

Nomothetic instruments include the following:

- Evaluation of Competency to Stand Trial–Revised (ECST-R)

- MacArthur Competence Assessment Tool–Criminal Adjudication (MacCAT-CA) the scale scores are *not* summed to total one final score for the ECST-R, and no cut-offs are used to determine whether a defendant is competent or incompetent. As with every other competency assessment instrument, information obtained with the ECST-R is used in conjunction with various other sources of information in the evaluation of an individual's competence to stand trial.

The ECST-R demonstrates high internal consistency, with α-coefficients for the competency scales ranging from .83 to .89 and α-coefficients for the feigning scales ranging from .63 to .87. Interrater reliability for the ECST-R scales ranged from .91 to 1.00 (Rogers, Grandjean, Tillbrook, Vitacco, & Sewell, 2001; Rogers, Tillbrook, & Sewell, 2004).

The MacArthur Competence Assessment Tool—Criminal Adjudication
The MacCAT-CA (Hoge, Bonnie, Poythress, & Monahan, 1999; Poythress et al., 1999) was developed between 1989 and 1996 by the MacArthur Foundation Research Network on Mental Health and the Law. The MacCAT-CA consists of 22 items grouped into three sections that measure a defendant's understanding, reasoning, and appreciation abilities, respectively. Administration time is approximately 30 minutes. The examiner begins by reading a hypothetical vignette, which serves as the basis for the first two sections (16 items); the third section asks questions related to the defendant's specific case. The vignette describes a bar fight between two men, Fred and Reggie, which results in an aggravated assault charge against Fred. The defendant is asked a series of questions about Fred's situation and how Fred might deal with various aspects of his case. More details of the vignette are provided as the examiner moves through the first two sections of the MacCAT-CA.

The first section (eight items) assesses the defendant's ability to *understand* information about the legal system and the legal process. For each item, the defendant is asked a question related to the vignette (e.g., "What is the job of the attorney for the defense") and is awarded 2 points (items are rated 0, 1, 2) if he is able to answer the question in a manner that demonstrates full understanding. If the defendant earns less than 2 points, the examiner discloses the answer and asks the defendant to repeat the disclosure in his own words. The purpose of the disclosure is to assess separately the defendant's *capacity* to understand apart from his *actual* or preexisting understanding. This provides an evaluation of the information the defendant knew without prompting and the capacity of the defendant to acquire and process new information.

The second section (eight items) assesses the defendant's ability to *reason*. The first five items in this section assess the defendant's ability to consider two pieces of factual information related to the vignette and identify the most important or legally relevant piece of information that one should disclose to a lawyer. The last three items require the defendant to think through mock legal options (relevant to the vignette) and to evaluate them in various ways.

The final section (six items) assesses the defendant's ability to *appreciate* her own legal circumstances and situation. This section departs from the hypothetical vignette format to explore the defendant's beliefs and perceptions about her personal role as a defendant and how she will be treated during the course of adjudication. These items are scored on the basis of the reasons that the defendant provides for her judgment and whether they are plausible or implausible (i.e., grounded in reality or based on delusional beliefs). The manual provides clear scoring criteria for each of the three sections and information regarding when additional prompts are necessary.

The authors of the MacCAT-CA emphasize that this instrument was developed for use as a tool rather than a test of competence. That is, the results do not indicate that a person *is* or *is not* competent. Rather, the scores obtained must be interpreted within the context of the specific defendant's case and integrated with all the other clinically relevant factors and information collected by the evaluator.

The psychometric properties of the MacCAT-CA were examined based on a sample of 729 felony defendants in eight different states (Otto et al., 1998; see also Rogers et al., 2001). The results indicated that the MacCAT-CA demonstrated good reliability. For each of the three sections, internal consistency ranged from .81 to .88 (α = .81 for Reasoning, .85 for Understanding, .88 for Appreciation) and interrater reliability ranged from very good to excellent (intraclass R = .75 for Appreciation, .85 for Reasoning, .90 for Understanding).

Otto and colleagues (1998) reported that additional support for the construct validity of the MacCAT-CA was "found in the pattern of correlations between the MacCAT-CA measures and select clinical variables" (p. 439). MacCAT-CA Understanding, Reasoning, and Appreciation scores correlated .41, .34, and .14, respectively, with estimated Wechsler Adult Intelligence Scale—Revised (WAIS-R) full-scale IQ, and $-.23$, $-.29$, and $-.36$, respectively, with Brief Psychiatric Rating Scale (BPRS) total scores (these scores correlated more strongly with BPRS Psychoticism and Emotional Withdrawal than with Depression and Hostility scales). The three MacCAT-CA scales correlated moderately with clinicians' global ratings of competency (r = .36, .42, and .49, respectively).

Zapf, Skeem, and Golding (2005) conducted a confirmatory factor analysis of the MacCAT-CA using the original norming database (n = 729). They found that a three-factor model, which corresponded to the three sections of the MacCAT-CA, was a reasonably good fit of the data; however, they determined that a modified three-factor model provided a better fit. Zapf and colleagues noted that,

> The method of measurement is somewhat confounded with the facet of competency measured. Specifically, the first factor in the modified model was composed of items that addressed vignette-based understanding (including legal options); the second factor, case-specific items that addressed specific appreciation; and the third factor, vignette-based items that required identification of the more relevant of two pieces of information. (p. 442)

Zapf and colleagues' comment regarding their finding that method variance may be confounded with construct variance is consistent with prior research (Rogers et al., 2001), which found that the vignette-based items on the MacCAT-CA loaded separately from the case-specific inquiries.

IDIOGRAPHIC INSTRUMENTS

The Fitness Interview Test–Revised The FIT (Roesch, Webster, & Eaves, 1984) was originally created in 1984 to assess fitness to stand trial in Canada. It has since been extensively revised to reflect issues and considerations relevant in both Canada (FIT-R; Roesch, Zapf, Eaves, & Webster, 1998) and the United States (FIT-R; Roesch, Zapf, & Eaves, 2006). The FIT-R focuses on the psycholegal abilities of the defendant and uses a 3-point rating scale: a score of 2 indicates definite or serious impairment; 1 indicates possible or mild impairment; and 0 indicates no impairment. The items on the FIT-R were developed to parallel the standards for fitness that were established in the Criminal Code of Canada as well as the Federal standard for competence to stand trial used in the United States (U.S. Code Annotated, Title 18, Part III, chapter 13, section 4241).

The FIT-R takes approximately 30 minutes to administer and uses a semi-structured interview format to assess three main areas:

1. the ability to understand the nature or object of the proceedings, or factual knowledge of criminal procedure;

2. the ability to understand the possible consequences of the proceedings, or the appreciation of personal involvement in and importance of the proceedings; and

3. the ability to communicate with counsel, or to participate in the defense.

Each of these three sections is broken down into specific questions that tap into different areas involved in competence to proceed. The first section assesses the defendant's understanding

INFO

Idiographic instruments include the following:

- The Fitness Interview Test–Revised (FIT; FIT-R)

- The Interdisciplinary Fitness Interview (IFI; IFI-R)

- Georgia Court Competency Test (GCCT)

- Competency Assessment Instrument (CAI)

- Competency Screening Test (CST)

of the arrest process, the nature and severity of current charges, the role of key players, legal processes, pleas, and court procedure. The second section assesses the defendant's appreciation of the range and nature of possible penalties, appraisal of available legal defenses, and appraisal of likely outcome. The final section assesses the defendant's capacity to communicate facts to the lawyer, relate to the lawyer, plan legal strategy, engage in his own defense, challenge prosecution witnesses, testify relevantly, and manage courtroom behavior.

Research has indicated that the FIT-R appears to have adequate psychometric properties. Viljoen, Roesch, and Zapf (2002a) found the interrater reliability of the FIT-R to be high across psychologists, psychiatrists, nurses, and graduate students in psychology. Specifically, intraclass correlation coefficients ranged from .98 to 1.00 across groups of professionals (or .63 to 1.00 across single raters from professional groups). The mean intraclass correlation coefficients for most items on the FIT-R fell within the .80 and .90 range, when based on the full sample of raters.

Research indicates that the FIT-R demonstrates excellent utility as a screening instrument. In two studies, Zapf, Roesch, and Viljoen (2001) compared the results of a FIT-R-based competency evaluation with an institution-based evaluation. Hospital evaluators were blind to the results of the FIT-R evaluation. Each study used a sample of 100 defendants referred for competency evaluations who were interviewed by one of several clinical psychology doctoral students. Each study also evaluated the utility of a particular measure of mental status. In the first study, the FIT-R was combined with the Structured Clinical Interview for DSM-III-R–Patient Edition (SCID-P; Spitzer, Williams, Gibbon, & First, 1990). Agreement between FIT-R-based evaluations and hospital evaluations occurred in 87 cases (85 agreements of competence; two agreements of incompetence); thus, overall agreement was 87%. Disagreement occurred in 13 cases—two in which the FIT-R-based evaluation indicated competence but the hospital evaluation indicated incompetence. Thus, the false-negative rate was 2%. There were 11 cases in which the FIT-R-based evaluation resulted in a decision that the defendant was incompetent but the hospital evaluation determined the defendant to be competent. Thus, the false-positive rate was 11%. In the second study, the FIT-R was used in conjunction with the Brief Psychiatric Rating Scale (BPRS; Overall & Gorham, 1962). Methodology was the same as for the first study, except defendants in the second study were chosen on the basis of their active psychotic symptoms, so as to increase the potential rate of incompetence in the sample. Results of the FIT-R-based evaluation and the hospital evaluation were in agreement for 74 defendants—66 agreements of competence and eight agreements of incompetence; thus, the overall rate of agreement was 74%. Disagreement occurred in 26 cases—in two, the FIT-R-based evaluation found the defendant competent, but the hospital-based evaluation found the defendant incompetent. Thus, again, the false-negative rate was 2%. The other 24 cases of disagreement were in the opposite direction (FIT-R indicated incompetence but hospital indicated competence); thus, the false-positive rate was 24%.

Taken together, these two studies indicate that using the FIT-R as a screen for competency would have resulted in avoiding lengthier evaluations in all but 45 cases. Thus, instead of 200 referrals for inpatient evaluation, only 45 would have been referred. It is of interest to highlight the differences between decisions based on the FIT-R/SCID-P with decisions based on the FIT-R/BPRS. The FIT-R focuses on legal issues but, as previously discussed, an assessment of mental status is essential in order to reach a decision about a defendant's competency. The FIT-R/SCID-P interview took an average of 90 minutes to complete, compared to 30 minutes for the FIT-R/BPRS. Both the SCID-P and the BPRS did a good job of screening the vast majority of cases; therefore, jurisdictions considering use of the FIT-R as a screening instrument are left to decide whether the additional time and cost of the SCID-P is worthwhile.

It should also be noted that the false-positive rates reported in these two studies do not necessarily indicate that the initial decision was "incorrect." The average length of hospitalization was 23 days for Study 1 and 22 days for Study 2. Since the FIT-R-based evaluation was conducted within a few days of admission, it is likely that some of the defendants were initially incompetent but became competent as their situation changed during the course of the inpatient evaluation (almost all defendants were treated with psychotropic medication during their evaluation stay).

Evidence for the construct validity of the FIT-R was reported by Zapf and Roesch (2001), who found reasonably high agreement (chance-corrected $\kappa = .51$) between the FIT-R and the MacCAT-CA. In addition, the FIT-R has been shown to correlate positively with intelligence scores and psychotic symptoms (Viljoen, Roesch, & Zapf, 2002b; Viljoen, Zapf, & Roesch, 2003).

The Interdisciplinary Fitness Interview The IFI was designed to assess both the legal and psychopathological aspects of competency (Golding, Roesch, & Schreiber, 1984). The original IFI was comprised of three major sections:

1. legal issues (five items);
2. psychopathological issues (11 items); and
3. overall evaluation (four items).

Each of the items represents an organizing scheme for more specific subdomains that have influenced competency decisions. For example, six subdomains are subsumed under the broad "capacity to appreciate," which forms the core of item 1. These are

1. appreciating the nature of the state's criminal allegation;
2. having the ability to provide a reasonable account of one's behavior prior to, during, and subsequent to the alleged crime;
3. having the ability to provide an account of relevant others during the same time period;
4. having the ability to provide relevant information about one's own state of mind at the time of the

alleged crime, including intentions, feelings, and cognitions;

5. having the ability to provide information about the behavior of the police during apprehension, arrest, and interrogation; and

6. having the projected ability to provide feedback to an attorney about the veracity of witness testimony during trial, if a trial is likely to be involved.

Note, however, in line with the open-textured nature of the competency construct, that a complete enumeration is not possible; rather, an attempt is made to summarize the general "lay of the land," allowing for specifics to be a matter of personal judgment.

The IFI was designed so that evaluators would have to consider both legal and mental status issues, but neither in isolation. Indeed, the developers of the IFI recommended that, ideally, the interview would be conducted jointly by a mental health professional and an attorney. The format of the IFI requires evaluators to relate their observations to the specific demands of the legal situations. Items are scored on a 3-point scale, ranging from 0 ("no or minimal incapacity") to 2 ("substantial incapacity"). For each item, evaluators are asked to rate the degree of incapacity of the defendant, and to give the item a score, also on a 3-point scale, to indicate the influence that the incapacity might have on the overall decision about competency. Thus, a defendant may receive a score indicating the presence of hallucinations (item 10) but receive a low weight score because the evaluator has determined that the presence of hallucinations would not have much effect on the conduct of the legal case. Another defendant with the same symptom may receive a high weight score because the hallucinations are considered to be more of a potential problem during the legal proceedings.

Golding and colleagues (1984) used the IFI in a study of pretrial defendants in the Boston area who were referred by court clinics to a state mental hospital for competency evaluation. Defendants were interviewed by a two-person team composed of a lawyer and either a psychologist or a social worker. Although the interviews were conducted jointly, each evaluator independently completed the IFI rating form. Results demonstrated that judgments about competency could be made in a reliable manner by lawyers and mental health professionals. These two groups were in agreement on 97% of their final determinations of competency (58 defendants were considered competent, 17 incompetent, and disagreement occurred in the remaining two cases).

The IFI has been revised (Golding, 1993) to reflect changes in constitutional law and the adoption by many states of "articulated" competency standards (e.g., Utah, 1994). In its current form, the Interdisciplinary Fitness Interview-Revised (IFI-R) taps 31 relatively specific psycholegal abilities organized into 11 global domains. The IFI-R was developed on the original model used by Golding and colleagues (1984), but was altered to reflect a decade of experience, numerous court opinions, and the accumulated professional literature on competency assessments. For example, the IFI-R specifically addresses the issue of the iatrogenic effects of psychotropic medications (*Riggins v. Nevada*, 1992), a defendant's decisional competence to engage in rational choice about trial strategies, proceeding *pro se* or pleading guilty, and competence to confess. It was developed to mirror Utah's (1994) articulated competency code, which mandates that examiners address its 11 global domains, but should also apply to other jurisdictions. A revised and comprehensive training manual is available from the author (Golding, 1993).

The Georgia Court Competency Test   The GCCT was originally developed by Wildman and colleagues (1978) as a screening device to filter out those defendants who were clearly competent. It has since gone through a number of revisions (see Bagby, Nicholson, Rogers, & Nussbaum, 1992; Johnson & Mullett, 1987; Nicholson, Briggs, & Robertson, 1988; Wildman, White, & Brandenburg, 1990). The original version consisted of 17 items; the most common revised version, referred to as the Mississippi State Hospital Revision (GCCT-MSH), consists of 21 items. The first seven items of the GCCT-MSH require the defendant to

visually identify the location of certain participants in the courtroom (i.e., defendants are shown a drawing of a courtroom and
asked "where does the Judge sit?"). This is then followed by questions related to the function of certain individuals in the courtroom
(such as witnesses and lawyers), the nature of the charges that the
defendant is facing, how the defendant would assist her lawyer, the
nature of her relationship with the lawyer, and the consequences of
a guilty verdict. Each item is assigned both a weight and a rating.

Research on the GCCT-MSH has indicated that this instrument
displays high levels of reliability and validity (Nicholson, Robertson,
Johnson, & Jensen, 1988). Three factors were identified by
Nicholson and colleagues (1988)—Courtroom Layout, General
Legal Knowledge, and Specific Legal Knowledge—and these were
later replicated by Bagby and colleagues (1992). It was later suggested that this three-factor solution might only be appropriate for
defendants who were ordered to undergo assessment at the pretrial
stage since a two-factor solution (Legal Knowledge and Courtroom
Layout) was found to be more appropriate for defendants who had
been adjudicated incompetent and who were undergoing inpatient
treatment to restore competence (Ustad, Rogers, Sewell, &
Guarnaccia, 1996). The major drawback of the GCCT-MSH is that
it focuses upon foundational competencies and ignores the more
important decisional competencies (Zapf & Viljoen, 2003).

The Competency Assessment Instrument   The CAI (Laboratory of
Community Psychiatry, 1973; McGarry & Curran, 1973) was
developed by McGarry and his colleagues in the late 1960s. It uses
a semi-structured interview to obtain information to score 13
items related to legal issues. The items include "appraisal of available legal defenses," "quality of relating to attorney," "capacity to
disclose pertinent facts," and "capacity to testify relevantly." Each
item is scored on a 5-point scale, ranging from "total incapacity"
to "no incapacity." The CAI manual contains clinical examples of
levels of incapacity as well as suggested interview questions.

The CAI has been used in a number of jurisdictions, although
perhaps more as an interview-structuring device than in the two-
stage screening manner (with the CST) as originally intended by

McGarry (see Laben, Kashgarian, Nessa, & Spencer, 1977; Schreiber, 1978). Unfortunately, few studies report either reliability or validity data. Roesch and Golding (1980) used the CAI in a North Carolina study. Thirty interviews conducted by pairs of interviewers yielded item percent agreement ranging from 68.8% to 96.7%, with a median of 81.2%. The interviewers were in agreement on the competency status of 29 of the 30 defendants (26 competent, three incompetent). The interviewers' decisions were in concordance with the more lengthy hospital evaluation decisions in 27 of 30 cases (90%). In subsequent studies (Golding et al., 1984; see also a summary of research in Nicholson & Kugler, 1991), the CAI has shown high levels of *trained* interexaminer agreement and examiner–outcome agreement.

The Competency Screening Test   The CST was created by Lipsitt, Lelos, and McGarry (1971) as a screening measure to identify clearly competent defendants and thus minimize the need for lengthy inpatient evaluations. The CST is a 22-item measure in sentence completion format. Representative items are "Jack felt that the judge ___," or "If the jury finds me guilty ___." Defendants are asked to fill in the blanks to complete the sentence. Each item is given a score of 2 (competent), 1 (questionable), or 0 (incompetent). The CST was designed so that a low total score (Lipsitt and colleagues used a cutoff score of 20) would identify possible incompetent defendants, who would then be referred for further assessment.

The scoring method has been criticized (Brakel, 1974; Roesch & Golding, 1980) because of its idealized perception of the criminal justice system. On one item, "Jack felt that the judge ___," responses such as "was right" or "was fair" would receive a score of 2, while responses such as "was unjust," "was too harsh," or "was wrong" would get a score of zero. On another item, "when Bob disagreed with his lawyer on his defense, he ___," a score of zero would be given to "figured there was no sense arguing." Roesch and Golding (1980) suggested that such responses might actually reflect a sense of powerlessness in controlling one's outcome in the legal system, which may be based in part on past experiences with the legal system and may well be an accurate interpretation.

The CST can be scored reliably (Randolph, Hicks, & Mason, 1981), and studies comparing classification based on CST cutoff scores and hospital evaluation decisions reveal that it has a false-positive rate ranging from about 14% to 28%; thus, it tends to identify many individuals as incompetent who are later determined to be competent in hospital evaluations (Lipsitt et al., 1971; Nottingham & Mattson, 1981; Randolph et al., 1981; Shatin, 1979). False-positive errors are considered acceptable in screening instruments since the consequence of this error is simply further evaluation, but it is desirable to avoid high false-positive rates in order to minimize unnecessary evaluations. Psychometrically, it is most desirable to minimize false-negative errors, as these errors result in a possibly incompetent defendant being returned to trial. Most studies have found the false-negative rate of the CST to be low, although Roesch and Golding (1980) reported a false-negative rate of nearly 24% in their North Carolina study. The ideal screening instrument has a low false-positive rate and a close to zero false-negative rate.

The results of these studies suggest a mixed review of the CST. Although it appears that the CST is a reliable instrument, serious questions can be raised about its usefulness as a screening device because of the potential for misclassifying possibly incompetent defendants. Further, as Melton and colleagues (2007) comment, higher illiteracy rates and lower intellectual functioning in offender samples may present difficulties for the written administration of the CST. In addition, it does not directly assess the three prongs of the *Dusky* standard.

SPECIAL POPULATIONS

The Competence Assessment for Standing Trial for Defendants with Mental Retardation.   The CAST*MR (Everington, 1990; Everington & Luckasson, 1992) was developed to assess competence with mentally retarded defendants. The items of the CAST*MR were derived from a review of relevant literature, case law, and existing CST assessment instruments (Everington, 1990). The CAST*MR comprises 50 questions, administered orally to the defendant. The questions are divided into three sections that address the basic elements of the *Dusky* standard. Section I, Basic Legal Concepts, includes

25 multiple-choice items that address concepts related to the criminal trial process (e.g., the roles of the judge, a jury, the prosecutor, and defense attorney) and terms that are critical to the trial process (e.g., felony, plea bargain, and probation). Section II, Skills to Assist Defense, comprises 15 multiple-choice items that address the attorney–client relationship. Items on Sections I and II are scored as either correct (1 point) or incorrect (0 points). Section III, Understanding Case Events, consists of 10 open-ended questions designed to assess the defendant's ability to describe the relevant circumstances of his offense. Items are scored as 1 point, $1/2$ point, or 0 points based on the ability of the individual to relay information to his case in an accurate and understandable manner (Everington & Luckasson, 1992).

The CAST*MR was developed to assist in the determination of whether a defendant with mental retardation is competent to stand trial. The authors of the CAST*MR emphasize its use as only one component of an overall assessment. Results of the CAST*MR should be considered in the context of other relevant information (e.g., interviews, observations, social history) (Everington & Luckasson, 1992).

Two studies have been conducted to examine the psychometric properties of the CAST*MR. The results indicated that the instrument has good reliability and validity. Reliability and validity findings were similar to those found with other competency assessment instruments (Everington, 1990; Everington & Dunn, 1995). Results from the first study demonstrated that the internal consistency of the CAST*MR total score was .93 when estimated by Cronbach's α and .92 when estimated by the Kuder-Richardson (KR) method (Everington, 1990). The results from the second study were consistent with the first study. Internal consistency of the total score, using the Kuder-Richardson method, was estimated between .92 for KR formula 20 and .92 for KR formula 21. These findings indicate that the CAST*MR has a high level of homogeneity (Everington & Dunn, 1995). Using the Pearson product moment correlation, test-retest reliability was estimated twice at .89 and .90 (Everington, 1990; Everington & Dunn, 1995). Interrater reliability for Section III was estimated between 80% and 87% (Everington & Dunn, 1995).

Assessment Practices

Evaluation Settings

Until as recently as the 1980s, virtually all competency evaluations took place in inpatient settings. As we have indicated in our review of competency assessment instruments, a number of screening measures are now available that can be used to conduct brief assessments of defendants. Many evaluations now take place in community-based settings, including jails and mental health centers (see Fitzgerald, Peszke, & Goodwin, 1978; Melton, Weithorn, & Slobogin, 1987; Ogloff & Roesch, 1992; Roesch & Ogloff, 1996). As Grisso, Coccozza, Steadman, Fisher, and Greer (1994) commented, "the traditional use of centrally located, inpatient facilities for obtaining pretrial evaluations survives in only a minority of states, having been replaced by other models that employ various types of outpatient approaches" (p. 388).

Surveys of Current Practices

Borum and Grisso (1995, 1996) surveyed forensic psychologists and psychiatrists with at least five years of experience in conducting forensic evaluations, the majority of whom were board-certified, regarding their professional practices and psychological test usage in evaluations of competence to stand trial and criminal responsibility. In terms of the types of information that these professionals considered to be key elements of competency evaluation reports, the following were considered to be essential by the majority of evaluators:

1. basic identifying information about the defendant and the methods used in the evaluation, including the criminal charges, the date and place of the evaluation, and description of the purpose of the evaluation and the limits of confidentiality;

2. clinical data information, such as psychiatric history, current mental status, and current use of psychotropic medication; and

3. psycholegal information, including the defendant's understanding of the charges/penalties and the

possible pleas, the defendant's appreciation of the consequences of accepting a plea bargain or entering a guilty plea, the defendant's understanding of the roles of trial participants and her ability to communicate with and consider the advice of legal counsel, as well as the defendant's capacity for self-control and her ability to make decisions and process information without distortion due to mental illness.

Borum and Grisso (1996) also found that the experts considered it important to include certain opinions, such as the presence or absence of mental illness or mental retardation, and the expert's reasoning regarding the relationship between mental illness or mental retardation and the observed deficits in psycholegal abilities. In addition, the majority of experts rated as "important" the inclusion of a description of the situational circumstances in which the defendant's deficits might be more or less likely to compromise his participation. Less agreement was found with respect to whether an ultimate opinion regarding the defendant's competence should be offered, with about one-half of the experts endorsing this practice, whereas about 13% said ultimate opinions should not be included. Other experts reported that it did not matter, as fact-finders were not obligated to accept an expert's opinion. (This issue is discussed further in Chapter 7 of this book.) Another area of disagreement pertained to whether a defendant's description of the alleged offense should be included in the report. About one-half of the psychologists and one-third of the psychiatrists stated that it should not be included. (This issue is discussed further in Chapter 5 of this book.)

With regard to psychological testing, Borum and Grisso (1995) found that only 16% of psychiatrists and 29% of psychologists thought that testing was essential; however, the majority in each group agreed that psychological testing was either recommended or essential, with 56% reporting they used psychological tests "almost always" (in more than 80% of their cases) or "frequently" (in 41–80% of their cases). The most commonly used tests were the Minnesota Multiphasic Personality Inventory (MMPI-2; Hathaway

& McKinley, 1989) and the Wechsler Adult Intelligence Scale-Revised (WAIS-R; Wechsler, 1981) or other intellectual/cognitive abilities tests. Projective tests and neuropsychological tests were used infrequently. Forensic assessment instruments specifically designed for competency evaluations were used almost always or frequently by about 40% of the experts, but about half said that they rarely or never used such instruments. The most commonly used instruments were the CAI and the CST. It is important to keep in mind, however, that this survey was conducted over a decade ago, at a time when many of the competency assessment instruments that are available today were still being developed. A more recent survey of forensic evaluators' psychological test use in juvenile competency evaluations indicates that use of competency assessment instruments has increased since Borum and Grisso's original survey (see Ryba, Cooper, & Zapf, 2003).

3
chapter

APPLICATION

Preparation for the Evaluation

4

In this chapter, we outline the process of preparing for the evaluation of a defendant's competence to proceed. Before agreeing to participate as an evaluator in a competency assessment, however, a forensic mental health professional must ensure that he possesses the expertise to do so. Statutes with respect to competency evaluations vary by jurisdiction, with many jurisdictions specifically identifying the type of professional who may participate as an evaluator. As a general statement, most jurisdictions in the United States allow for a psychiatrist or a licensed psychologist to conduct competency evaluations. Some also allow for psychiatric social workers, psychiatric nurses or nurse practitioners, or other types of mental health professionals to act as evaluators. Thus, it is important to be familiar with the relevant legal statutes pertaining to competency evaluations in the particular jurisdiction in which the evaluation is requested.

Evaluator Preparation

Once it has been established that a mental health professional is legally eligible to participate as an evaluator in a competency assessment, it then must be determined whether she possesses the appropriate qualifications for the referral case.

Knowledge

Specific knowledge with respect to court procedure and legal doctrine

> **BEST PRACTICE**
>
> Ensure that you have the proper qualifications for the referral case, including the required
>
> - knowledge,
> - training,
> - skill set, and
> - experience.

is required before participating in forensic mental health assessment (FMHA). In addition, the evaluator must have knowledge regarding forensic psychology or psychiatry, as distinct from clinical psychology or general psychiatry. Given that there are differences in the ways in which individuals involved with the legal system should be evaluated (as compared to those who seek out psychological evaluation but are not involved with the legal system), the competent forensic practitioner should also have an understanding of these differences (see Greenberg & Shuman, 1997, for a discussion of the fundamental differences between clinical and forensic roles).

Training

In addition to general clinical training (clinical theories, assessment methods, diagnostic methods), specific training in the forensic realm is also necessary. That is, the forensic mental health professional should be trained in forensically relevant theories, assessment methods, and issues. This training may have been part of predoctoral education or be acquired through workshops, seminars, or other professional academic/training settings. In addition, some states require attendance at a training workshop on forensic assessment and forensic issues for those wishing to become or remain involved in FMHA work. Of course, the authors also strongly recommend that evaluators continue to enhance their skills and training through continuing education on forensic issues, regardless of whether this is required by the particular jurisdiction in which they practice (see Heilbrun, Grisso, & Goldstein, 2009, for a detailed discussion on training in forensic mental health practice). Evaluators should also stay abreast of the relevant legal statutes, case law, and administrative rules pertaining to forensic issues and evaluations in the jurisdictions in which they practice.

Skills

In addition to formal clinical and forensic training, it is also important for evaluators to have the requisite skills necessary to conduct forensic assessments. Many of the basic skills (interviewing, general assessment methods, diagnostic skills) will have been developed during predoctoral education and refined through pre- and postdoctoral clinical experience. Given the particular role of the forensic evaluator, however, specific forensic skills (administration and interpretation of forensic assessment instruments [FAIs], collateral information gathering) must also be acquired. The reader who is unfamiliar with the many important ways in which the forensic examiner's role differs from the role of the mental health professional in a therapeutic setting is referred to Greenberg and Shuman (1997), Heilbrun (2001), and Chapter 3 in Melton, Petrila, Poythress, and Slobogin (2007).

CULTURAL COMPETENCE

In addition to clinical and forensic skills, the evaluator must also be familiar with the various ways in which a defendant's racial, ethnic, social, and cultural background and experiences might impact upon her knowledge, skills, language, communication style, and test results. Culturally sensitive clinical and forensic practices are necessary to ensure fairness and accuracy in the evaluation context. A full discussion of cultural competence and culturally sensitive practices is beyond the scope of this book, but the reader is referred to Miller (2003), Tseng, Matthews, and Elwyn (2004), and Saldaña (2001) for a thorough discussion of these issues.

Experience

Closely associated with having the requisite skills for conducting forensic assessments is the need to obtain experience with this type of evaluation. Supervision of forensic work by competent and qualified forensic mental health professionals is an important

BEWARE The importance of obtaining the necessary training, skills, and experience cannot be understated, especially since the courts scrutinize these in considering whether to qualify an evaluator as an expert for the purposes of testifying about the results of a forensic assessment.

component of the learning process. It allows evaluators to obtain the necessary experience while working closely with someone who possesses the skills and experience that they seek. For mental health professionals working in state hospitals, forensic facilities, or group practices, it may be relatively easy to obtain consultation and supervision of clinical-forensic work. For those mental health professionals working in independent practice or academic settings, it may be more difficult, although no less important, to secure consultation and supervision of clinical-forensic work. Supervision of clinical-forensic work should continue until the mental health professional has enough skill and experience to be considered competent as per ethical and professional guidelines. (As will be discussed later in this chapter, the competent forensic evaluator should possess a high degree of familiarity with relevant ethical and professional guidelines; see American Psychological Association, 2002; Committee on Ethical Guidelines for Forensic Psychologists, 1991.) Consultation with other professionals about difficult cases or issues is part of professional practice and should occur on an ongoing basis as needed.

Clarifying the Referral

Depending upon the professional setting in which an evaluator practices, he may have more or less discretion to accept or decline particular referrals. Evaluators working in independent practice often have complete discretion to decide which referrals they will take on, whereas those working in state forensic facilities have little or no discretion. The evaluator needs to ensure that he will be able to conduct the assessment free of any bias or preconceived notions about the defendant or the nature of the case. The evaluator working in a private practice setting may simply decline the referral if objectivity may be compromised in a particular case.

The evaluator working in a state facility should discuss her concerns with a supervisor who may be able to reassign the case or with a colleague who may be able to trade cases.

Referral Question

Once the referral has been received, it is important to ascertain the specific referral question to be addressed in the evaluation. It is not uncommon for *court-ordered evaluations* to include incorrect or misleading information, such as confusing issues of competency with insanity. In addition, it may be that some attorneys are not familiar with the specific relevant legal statutes pertaining to competence to proceed and thus are unclear regarding the referral question.

Melton and colleagues (2007) specify three reasons regarding why it is important to clarify the referral question:

1. to ensure that the evaluator will be able to practice within the bounds of competence;

2. to ensure that expectations on the part of both the evaluator and the retaining attorney are understood, so as to minimize the possibility of conflict regarding the evaluation or testimony developing at some later point in time; and

3. to ensure that the evaluator will be able to provide all relevant information in the notification to the defendant regarding

    - the purpose and scope of the evaluation,

    - who will have access to the results of the evaluation,

    - and the limits on confidentiality of the information obtained during the course of the evaluation.

4
chapter

Referral Source

It is necessary to determine who has requested the evaluation, as well as the means by which the referral is made. That is, there is an

BEST PRACTICE
Understand who is requesting the evaluation, as well as who is retaining your services.

important distinction to be made between a court-ordered evaluation and a private (*ex parte*) evaluation.

In a court-ordered evaluation, regardless of which party may have initiated the request for the assessment, the forensic evaluator is working for the court. Therefore, the evaluator must exercise caution with respect to any communications with defense and prosecution, so as not to give the impression that she is favoring one side over the other. In addition, in court-ordered evaluations, a written report will always be necessary.

In *ex parte* evaluations, the forensic evaluator will be retained by either the prosecution or the defense, and therefore will communicate mainly with the retaining attorney. In addition, the retaining attorney should be consulted before the forensic evaluator engages in any discussions with the opposing attorney. Finally, in private evaluations, an initial verbal report is provided to the retaining party, who will then determine whether a written report is necessary. In those cases in which the opinion of the forensic evaluator is not helpful to the retaining attorney, a written report will usually not be requested. Thus, it is imperative that the forensic mental health professional understands who is requesting the evaluation and who is retaining her services.

In addition to clarifying the referral question and understanding who has requested the assessment and retained the expert, the forensic evaluator will need to obtain relevant background information from the referral source before he can proceed with the evaluation. Two pieces of information are crucial: information regarding the current charges/allegations (and the possible penalties); and information regarding why the issue of competency was raised. Information regarding the defendant's previous criminal history and experiences with court proceedings, while not crucial, is often helpful.

CURRENT CHARGES AND ALLEGATIONS

To conduct an assessment of a defendant's competence to proceed, the evaluator needs to know the current criminal charges that the defendant is facing, as well as some indication of the content of the allegations. The distinction between charges and allegations is an important one. The specific criminal charge or charges that the defendant is facing may not necessarily indicate to the evaluator the circumstances surrounding

the alleged offense. Thus, although it is important to know the formal charges that the defendant is facing, it is arguably more important to be aware of the nature of the allegations surrounding the charges. Having knowledge regarding the allegations will assist the evaluator in making a thorough assessment of the defendant's understanding and appreciation of the charges that she is facing. In addition, this information will provide the evaluator with specific knowledge about the case that may be useful in formulating questions to ascertain the defendant's competence-related abilities.

INFORMATION REGARDING REASON FOR REFERRAL

In addition to information regarding the current charges and allegations, the evaluator will also need to obtain information regarding the reason for the competency referral. Specifically, the evaluator will need to inquire about why the competency issue was raised. That is, what was it about the defendant or his behaviors or interactions with the referring party that resulted in the request for evaluation? As was discussed in Chapter 3, there can be many reasons why a competency referral is made, including the simple fact that the defendant has a history of mental illness. Therefore, it is important for evaluators to obtain information regarding the specific reason for referral in each case.

Evaluators who work in state forensic facilities or those who routinely perform court-ordered evaluations may find it useful to have the referring party submit a form with referral information regarding criminal charges, allegations, and the reasons for referral. Appendix A contains a modified version of a form originally developed by Kruh, Sullivan, and Dunham (2001) and adapted by Grisso (2005) for the purpose of collecting relevant information from the defense attorney. Evaluators who work in independent practice can collect relevant

4
chapter

referral information over the phone from the referring attorney during the initial referral contact. They will also want to request that the referring attorney provide copies of the arrest report, indictment, and other relevant documents.

CRIMINAL HISTORY AND PREVIOUS LEGAL EXPERIENCE

Information regarding the defendant's criminal history and her experiences with the legal system can usually be obtained from the retaining attorney. While not crucial for the evaluation of a defendant's CST, this information is useful for making a determination regarding her level of knowledge about court proceedings and court process.

Fee Arrangement/Negotiation

The fee structure for professional services should be clarified with the retaining attorney prior to commencement of the evaluation. If the evaluator is court-appointed, it will usually be the case that a predetermined fee for the evaluation as been set by the court. *Ex parte* evaluators will need to clarify the financial arrangements early on in their initial contacts with the retaining party. Discussions surrounding the fee structure should include information regarding whether a retainer is expected and when payment for services is due. In addition, the forensic evaluator should be aware that financial arrangements in which compensation is contingent upon the outcome of the case are not appropriate.

Attorney Representation

All defendants have a right to assistance of counsel. Thus, as a general rule, it is necessary to determine whether a defendant who has been ordered to undergo an evaluation of CST has had an opportunity to discuss this with his attorney. In most cases, this will be obvious as it will be the defense attorney who either requests the evaluation or retains the forensic examiner. It is conceivable, however, that the court may order a competency evaluation before the defendant has retained counsel or counsel has been appointed for the defendant. If this is the case, the evaluation should be postponed until counsel has been appointed and the defendant has had the opportunity to discuss the evaluation request with the defense attorney. Thus, the forensic evaluator is responsible for determining who the defendant's attorney is and for providing notification to the defense attorney regarding the fact that a competency evaluation has been ordered (if the defense attorney was not the one to request the evaluation or retain the evaluator).

> **BEST PRACTICE**
> Contact the defense attorney to provide notice of the evaluation and to obtain relevant information before meeting the defendant.

In general, it is useful for the forensic examiner to contact the defense attorney before meeting with the defendant. This ensures that the defense counsel is aware of the evaluation (if he was not the one to make the request or retain the evaluator) and allows the evaluator the opportunity to obtain information regarding the charges, allegations, possible penalties, possible defense strategies, and abilities required of the defendant to meet the contextual demands of the case before the evaluation interview.

Assistance in Obtaining Relevant Sources of Information

The defense attorney will be an important resource in terms of assisting the evaluator in obtaining relevant sources of information, including the following:

- arrest reports and/or indictments (to provide information regarding the charges as well as the allegations);

- information regarding previous criminal history and contacts with the legal system;

- information regarding possible penalties and possible defense strategies (to assist the evaluator in determining whether the defendant has a rational as well as factual understanding of these issues);

- information regarding the complexity of the case and the abilities required of the defendant to meet the demands of the case (to allow for a functional evaluation within the contextual nature of the case); and

- collateral contacts and other sources of information about the defendant.

If the defense attorney requested the competency assessment, the *ex parte* evaluator should be able to request this information during their initial or ongoing contact. If, however, the competency evaluation was court-ordered, and the evaluator is participating as an independent party, prolonged personal contacts with the defense attorney (such as phone calls) should be limited, and the relevant information should be requested in writing (see Appendix A). If the evaluator chooses to place a telephone call to the defense attorney to obtain relevant information (since this may be more timely than a written request), he should be aware of attempts by the attorney to influence the course and outcome of the evaluator and guard against these. Using a form, such as that presented in Appendix A, to structure the telephone call will assist in guarding against lengthy discussions about the defendant and the case.

Determining What Is Required of the Defendant

Since the defense attorney is the only party who knows what will be required of the defendant for the particular case, it is important to speak with him (or request this information in writing) to gain an understanding of the complexities of the case and the requirements of the defendant in participating or assisting in her defense. This is particularly important given that the evaluation of a defendant's competence to proceed should be conducted in a contextualized manner. As discussed in Chapter 2 and throughout this book, a functional assessment of competency requires that the evaluation take into account the specific demands of the case. For example, an evaluator's opinion regarding a defendant's competence-related abilities may hinge on whether that defendant will be required to testify. That is, it may be the case that, should the defendant be required to testify, the evaluator may opine that the individual is unable to assist in his defense, whereas the reverse may be true if the defendant is not required to testify.

Having the Defense Attorney Present

Although it is rare that defense attorneys are present during an evaluation, there may be occasions when a defendant requests the presence of her attorney. The courts have been inconsistent with respect to whether the defendant has a right to

> **BEST PRACTICE**
> Conduct a functional assessment of a defendant's abilities within the context of her particular case, including her ability to communicate with and assist counsel.

the presence of counsel during pretrial evaluations of competency (see Melton et al., 2007); however, Melton and colleagues (2007) recommend that defense counsel be permitted to observe the evaluation process when practicable. In some instances, especially in those cases wherein the competency evaluation has been requested by the defense, it may be necessary for the defense attorney to participate in, rather than simply observe, the evaluation. This would be particularly relevant when the defense attorney's relationship with the defendant is at issue in the determination of CST. Of course, participation by the defense attorney may also be relevant in court-ordered evaluations. In these cases, it is wise for the evaluator to approach the defense attorney beforehand, as he may not be willing to participate in court-ordered assessments.

When the evaluation is court-ordered, the defendant does not have the right to remain silent; thus, if present during the assessment, the defense attorney does not have the prerogative to direct the client not to answer certain questions. In this type of situation, it is best to have the defense attorney sit in a location that would allow her to observe, but not interfere with, the evaluation. In addition, it is always best for the evaluator to discuss the expectations ahead of time with the defense attorney, so that she is aware of the need to conduct the evaluation with little or no interference.

If the defense attorney wishes to be present at a court-ordered evaluation, and the logistics of scheduling then precludes conducting the evaluation in a timely manner, audio- or video-taping the evaluation may present an acceptable alternative.

Logistics of the Evaluation

Timeline

Ascertaining the timeline for the evaluation is an important aspect in preparing to conduct a competency evaluation. It is important to determine the stage at which the defendant is currently in the proceedings and whether the next court date has been set. Many jurisdictions will allow 30 days for a competency evaluation; however, the American Bar Association (1989) has recommended a period of 14 days when the defendant is on pretrial release and seven days when the defendant is in jail. Given the focus on the current functioning of the defendant, many competency evaluations can take place within a relatively short timeframe (as discussed in detail in Chapter 3). In some instances, however, the evaluator may need to request copies of relevant information required for the evaluation (see subsequent section on third-party or collateral information sources). This may involve having the defendant sign releases, so having sufficient time to obtain relevant information in this situation is paramount.

If the timeline is too short, and the evaluator does not believe that there is enough time to conduct a thorough evaluation, this should be communicated to the referral party, so that an extension might be obtained. If it is imperative that the evaluation occurs within a timeframe that does not allow for the collection of all relevant information, the evaluator should indicate in the report which records or information sources were requested but not received by the time of writing. This serves the purpose of acknowledging that some important information may not have been taken into consideration in rendering the opinions set forth in the report.

Setting

If the defendant is in jail, the evaluation usually takes place at the jail; however, some jurisdictions allow for the defendant to be transported to the evaluator's office or to an outpatient forensic facility for the purposes of the assessment. If the evaluation is to occur at the jail, the evaluator should inquire with the party requesting the evaluation about

BEST PRACTICE

Check that the timeline allows sufficient time to obtain all the relevant information for the evaluation.

whether any specific procedures must be followed to gain access to the defendant. Some
jails require the evaluator to be cleared by
security ahead of time (as much as two weeks
or more in advance), and some require an
appointment be set to see the defendant. In

> **BEST
> PRACTICE**
> Make sure the evaluation
> setting allows for enough
> privacy to adequately assess
> the defendant's functioning.

addition, the facilities available for an evaluation vary by jail. An
inquiry regarding whether an interview space is free for the particular time that the evaluator is to see the defendant may prove useful.

If the defendant is not in jail, he will usually be seen at the
evaluator's office (some jurisdictions provide the opportunity for
court-appointed community evaluators to see the defendant at a
forensic facility on an outpatient basis). It is important for the evaluator to keep track of the appointment that was set with the defendant. If the defendant does not show up for the appointment, the
evaluator should inform the party requesting the evaluation.

In some jurisdictions, the evaluation of competency may take
place on an inpatient basis at a forensic facility or state psychiatric
hospital. In this situation, the evaluator will be an employee of the
inpatient facility and, thus, access to the defendant is relatively easy.

As much as possible, the setting for the evaluation should be
quiet, private, and free from distraction. Of course, this may prove
difficult to obtain in some jails or pretrial facilities. At a minimum,
however, the setting should allow for privacy. If an evaluator finds
that the evaluation setting is not private and thus does not allow for
an adequate assessment of the defendant's functioning, she may
need to request that the evaluation occur in a different setting.

Authorization

Before conducting an evaluation of competency it is important for
the forensic mental health expert to obtain the appropriate authorization. For court-ordered evaluations, this authorization comes in
the form of a signed court order, a copy of which should be
obtained by the evaluator before proceeding. In this instance, the
evaluator need only provide the defendant with a notification of
purpose (discussed later); obtaining consent from the defendant is
not necessary.

BEST PRACTICE

Obtain proper authorization. For court-ordered evaluations,

● obtain a copy of the signed court order, and

● provide defendant with notification of purpose.

For *ex parte* evaluations,

● provide defendant with notification of purpose, and

● obtain consent of both the attorney and the client.

For defense-requested *ex parte* evaluations, proper authorization comes in the form of consent from both the attorney and the client. Thus, in addition to providing the defendant with a notification of purpose, informed consent must also be obtained. In some jurisdictions, when the evaluator is being retained privately by one party or the other (as opposed to the court more generally), a request for evaluation will be submitted to the court for approval and for payment authorization. This generally occurs only when the defense attorney has made a request for an evaluator of his choosing and is asking the court to pay for the evaluation. In these cases, it is wise, but not necessary, to wait for this approval before proceeding with the evaluation. When one does proceed, it is still necessary to obtain the consent of the attorney and the defendant.

Recording the Evaluation

Whether to record the evaluation, either via video or audio, is usually a matter for the evaluator to decide. In those cases in which the defense attorney has requested to be present at the evaluation, but for logistical reasons this is not feasible, recording the evaluation may be an appropriate alternative. There is no requirement to record the evaluation, except perhaps in those cases where it has been requested or court-ordered; however, recording the assessment provides the evaluator with a convenient record for subsequent review. This may be particularly helpful when preparing for a competency hearing wherein the evaluation took place months earlier or for clarifying specific procedures (or the duration of those procedures) that were used during the evaluation.

Use of Obtained Information

Every defendant has the right to remain silent so as not to provide information to the prosecution that would be self-incriminating; however, virtually every state allows for the prosecution to compel a defendant to undergo a competency evaluation once competency arises as an issue. Given that the focus of the competency evaluation is on the functional abilities required of the defendant, it is likely that the defendant may make self-incriminating statements during the evaluation.

The U.S. Supreme Court examined the issue of a defendant's Fifth Amendment right against self-incrimination in *Estelle v. Smith* (1981). In this case, the court-ordered pretrial competency evaluator, Dr. James Grigson, a psychiatrist, returned after the guilty verdict to testify about the defendant's dangerousness at the sentencing hearing of a death penalty trial. His testimony at sentencing, that the defendant would be a danger to society, was based on his pretrial competency evaluation of the defendant. The issue of whether the results of a competency evaluation could be used for the purposes of sentencing was brought before that Court. The U.S. Supreme Court decided that competency evaluation results should be limited to the issue of competency and that to enter this information into evidence at a sentencing hearing would violate a defendant's Fifth Amendment right against compelled self-incrimination. Thus, defendants do not have to participate in court-ordered competency evaluations unless the results are only used to determine competence. In addition to the constitutional protection offered by *Estelle,* many states also include statutory protection of the information obtained in a pretrial competency evaluation and limit its use to the issue of competency.

Regardless of the fact that there exists court-ordered or statutory protection against using the results of a competency evaluation at trial, evaluators must be careful to consider this issue when writing the competency evaluation report. Given the potential for prosecutorial misuse of incriminating information contained within the report, it appears that the best strategy is the most conservative. That is, evaluators should make general, process-oriented statements regarding whether the defendant was able or unable to

CASE LAW

Estelle v. Smith (1981)

● U.S. Supreme Court held that competency evaluation results should be limited to the issue of competency and not be used at trial.

perform specific tasks and regarding the abilities of the defendant, rather than statements regarding specific content. (See further discussion of this issue in Chapter 5.)

Scope and Focus of the Evaluation

Consulting Relevant Statutes

Every jurisdiction possesses legal statutes relevant to CST, although some contain more detailed information than others. It is crucial that evaluators consult the relevant legal statutes, case law, and administrative rules for the particular jurisdiction in which the evaluation is sought. Often, the legal statutes or administrative rules will contain information regarding the specific factors or criteria that must be addressed in either the assessment or the report, or both. In addition, these sources may detail any specific procedures that are to be followed in a competency evaluation. Some jurisdictions require evaluators who opine that a defendant is incompetent to proceed to include information regarding the condition causing incompetence, the types of treatment available to treat the condition, the facilities wherein the types of treatments may be offered, the prognosis for the individual, the likelihood that the individual will be able to be restored to competency, and the amount of time that will be necessary to restore an individual to competency.

Determining What Collateral Information Is Needed

As is the case with any type of forensic evaluation, collateral information must be sought to either confirm or disconfirm the defendant's account of events and self-report of relevant information. Given that the focus of a competency evaluation is on the defendant's current mental status and competence-related abilities, it may not be necessary in every evaluation to consult numerous collateral information sources. At a minimum, before meeting the defendant, the evaluator should obtain informa-

BEST PRACTICE
Be familiar with the jurisdictional requirements for the evaluation as well as for the content of the report.

tion regarding the charges and allegations, the possible penalties, the complexity of the case, and the abilities required
of the defendant. The complexity of the
case, as well as the characteristics of
the particular defendant, should guide
the evaluator in terms of additional collat-
eral information to be sought. Thus, collateral interviews with
family members or other individuals who have had close contact
with the defendant may be necessary in those cases in which the
evaluator requires more information about the current functioning of the defendant. Similarly, mental health records may
be sought in those cases in which the defendant has a documented history of mental illness, and the evaluator requires
more information regarding previous functioning to make a
judgment about current functioning. Records from the jail or
pretrial facility where the defendant is being detained may be
necessary in those cases in which the evaluator requires more
information about the defendant's current functioning when
the defendant does not believe he is being monitored. Potential
third-party or collateral information sources are listed
in Appendix B.

> **BEST PRACTICE**
> Be guided by the nature
> of the case and the
> presentation of the defendant
> in your search for collateral
> information.

Determining What Forensic Assessment Instruments to Use

The evaluator will need to make a determination regarding
whether to use FAIs during the course of the competency evaluation. Although no professional guidelines mandate the use of
FAIs for the purposes of a competency evaluation, a number of
such instruments have been developed, and empirical data
suggest that trained evaluators using FAIs achieve the highest
levels of interexaminer and examiner–adjudication agreement
(Golding, Roesch, & Schreiber, 1984; Nicholson & Kugler,
1991; Skeem, Golding, Cohn, & Berge, 1998). As elaborated in
Chapter 5, there are a number of advantages to using FAIs and
few limitations (to thoughtfully selected instruments). Thus, we
recommend the use of FAIs to guide the evaluation of CST.

4
chapter

Those instruments that have been developed to assist in the evaluation of CST have been discussed in Chapter 3. Suffice it to say that the evaluator should select an instrument on the basis of relevance and reliability, and should become familiar with the instrument before using it in an evaluation. (More discussion regarding the selection of an appropriate FAI can be found in Chapter 5.) One issue of concern is with regard to some of the competency assessment instruments being "harder" or "easier" than others. Thus, it might be possible for an evaluator to select an instrument for use in a specific case that would either increase or decrease the possibility of the defendant being considered incompetent. In response to this concern, we recommend that the evaluator select a FAI, such as the Fitness Interview Test–Revised (FIT-R) or the Interdisciplinary Fitness Interview–Revised (IFI-R), that can be utilized in *every* evaluation of CST to ensure adequate, consistent coverage of the relevant competency domains, and then supplement the evaluation with additional FAIs, such as the MacArthur Competence Assessment Tool–Criminal Adjudication (MacCAT-CA) or the Evaluation of Competency to Stand Trial– Revised (ECST-R), in those cases in which normative information regarding how the defendant compares to other defendants in terms of competence-related abilities is applicable and relevant. This ensures consistent coverage (both in terms of breadth and depth) of competence-related issues by the evaluator for every evaluation but also allows for supplementation of this information with additional instruments relevant to the specific situation.

In addition to FAIs for the purposes of evaluating competence-related abilities, the evaluator may also need to employ *forensically relevant instruments* (see Chapter 5) to assist in the evaluation of conditions (such as malingering response style or psychopathy) that need to be considered within the context of any forensic evaluation. The use of forensically relevant instruments will depend upon the nature of the case and the characteristics of the defendant. As with the selection of FAIs for

BEST PRACTICE

Select a reliable FAI to use in every competency evaluation, supplementing it with additional instruments as relevant for a specific case.

use as part of a CST evaluation, evaluators should be careful to select forensically relevant instruments on the basis of the reliability of the instrument and relevance to the particular issue to be evaluated (in this case, the issue would be something that may be related to the issue of CST—such as malingering—but not competence to stand trial *per se*).

Heilbrun, Marczyk, and DeMatteo (2002) state that the use of FAIs (developed to measure the capacities related to a particular legal question, such as CST) are preferable to conventional psychological tests for assessing functional legal capacities when the following criteria are met: "clear directions for administration, objective scoring criteria, quantification of the level or degree of performance, research on reliability and validity, and documentation in a manual" (p. 5).

Determining Whether Other Psychological Tests Are Necessary

It may be the case that, during a CST evaluation, a certain issue arises for which psychological testing may be useful. For example, there may be a concern about how the intellectual or emotional functioning of the defendant impacts the defendant's competence-related abilities. In these instances, it is important for the evaluator to select psychological tests that are relevant to the specific legal inquiry (i.e., CST). That is, a link must exist between the particular issue at hand and the defendant's competence-related abilities. In addition, Melton and colleagues (2007) as well as Heilbrun and colleagues (2002) recommend that psychological test results be treated as hypotheses to be verified through other sources (such as third-party interviews or collateral information sources). Finally, the psychological tests selected should be *face valid*. That is, they should *appear* to be accurate measures of the indicated capacities, as well as actually *be* accurate measures of those capacities.

BEST PRACTICE

If psychological tests are necessary to provide additional information about a particular competence-related capacity,

- be sure the testing is relevant to the specific legal inquiry (CST),

- select tests that are face valid, and

- verify the test results through other sources.

4
chapter

Since CST deals with a defendant's mental state at the present point in time, any psychological tests used should accurately reflect the defendant's present mental state, rather than her mental state at an earlier time. Thus, previous psychological testing may not be relevant to the current assessment of competence. In rare instances, evaluators may be asked to reconstruct a defendant's previous mental state to determine whether that individual was competent at that point in time, such as when she may have waived her *Miranda* rights. In these cases, the role of psychological tests that reflect the defendant's present mental state may have limited utility in attempting to reconstruct her mental state at some earlier time.

It is not necessary to use traditional psychological tests as part of a standard battery of testing in CST evaluations; in fact, we would argue that it is only necessary in those cases in which the evaluator requires additional information about a particular capacity that may impact upon the defendant's competence-related abilities. In those instances, it may be useful for the evaluator to select psychological tests that are relevant to the particular capacity to be assessed, then tie the results to the defendant's competence-related functioning. Selected tests should be reliable (in terms of their psychometric properties) and valid (in terms of their measuring what they purport to measure). Thus, the evaluator may wish to make a list of the capacities for which more information need be sought and select the best, most appropriate, psychological tests for measuring those capacities. Obviously, this will need to be done on a case-by-case basis, usually after interviewing the defendant.

In terms of assisting mental health professionals in determining whether a particular psychological test should be used in a forensic evaluation, Heilbrun (1992) provides the following guidelines:

1. The test is commercially available and adequately documented in two sources. First, it is accompanied by a manual describing its development, psychometric properties,

and procedure for administration. Second, it is listed in *Mental Measurements Yearbook* or some other readily available source.

2. Reliability should be considered. The use of tests with a reliability coefficient of less than .80 is not advisable. The use of less reliable tests would require an explicit justification by the psychologist.

3. The test should be relevant to the legal issue, or to a psychological construct underlying the legal issue. Whenever possible, this relevance should be supported by the availability of validation research published in refereed journals.

4. Standard administration should be used, with testing conditions as close as possible to the quiet, distraction-free ideal.

5. Applicability to this population and for this purpose should guide both test selection and interpretation. The results of a test (distinct from behavior observed during testing) should not be applied toward a purpose for which the test was not developed (e.g., inferring psychopathology from the results of an intelligence test). Population and situation specificity should guide interpretation. The closer the "fit" between a given individual and the population and situation of those used in the validation research, the more confidence can be expressed in the applicability of the results.

6. Objective tests and actuarial data combinations are preferable when appropriate outcome data and a "formula" exist.

7. Response style should be explicitly assessed using approaches sensitive to distortion and the results of psychological testing interpreted within the context of the individual's response style. When response style appears to be malingering, defensive, or irrelevant, rather than honest or reliable, the results of psychological testing may need to be discounted or even ignored and other data sources emphasized to a greater degree.

(pp. 264–267)

4
chapter

Collateral Information

Preparing to Obtain Relevant Collateral Information

Once the evaluator has determined the third-party or collateral information sources that are relevant to the particular defendant's case, she must go about the business of obtaining these pieces of data for inclusion in the evaluation. The usual means of obtaining access to this information is through the referring party. The *ex parte* evaluator should work with the retaining attorney (usually the defense attorney) to collect the relevant pieces of information. When the evaluation is court-ordered, it is necessary for the evaluator to work through the court to obtain this information. This is usually easiest to do by sending a letter to the defense attorney, with a copy to the prosecuting attorney and the judge who ordered the competency evaluation, asking for the relevant records (these should be listed in the letter). It may also be necessary to include release of information forms to be signed by the defendant, which can be sent to the party or institution in possession of the information.

Making direct contact with third parties or those in possession of collateral records should be a last resort of the evaluator. The *ex parte* evaluator should be aware that legal ethics prohibit directly contacting persons represented by counsel; thus, one must be careful not to contact parties (as opposed to witnesses) to the proceedings. If necessary, Melton and colleagues (2007) suggest that the evaluator remind the referring party who balks at providing assistance that a report will not be forthcoming until all necessary data have been obtained. Another alternative is to provide an incomplete report, with a note detailing the reasons for its incompleteness.

RECORDS

BEWARE
Do not directly contact persons represented by counsel, as this goes against legal ethics.

To obtain relevant medical, mental health, academic, institutional, or other types of records, it will usually be necessary to have the defendant sign a release of information form, which is then sent to the relevant agency with a request for the records. This is usually easiest done by sending the release forms to the retaining attorney with instructions to have the defendant sign and then send the forms to the relevant agency to obtain the records. To expedite the process, the evaluator may want to include instructions on the release of information forms to have the records sent directly to her office.

INTERVIEWS

To obtain interviews with relevant individuals, the examiner should request that the retaining attorney put him in contact with those individuals believed to be important and relevant sources of third-party information. Upon contacting these individuals, the examiner should be clear about the purpose of the evaluation and his role as either court-appointed or *ex parte* evaluator. In some instances, it may be appropriate for the evaluator to contact individuals directly, without going through the retaining attorney; however, these contacts should probably be reserved to those situations where its permissibility has been established through custom or common sense (such as contacting the mental health professionals or other personnel at the jail where the defendant is being held).

Ethical Issues

Confidentiality

Although the issue of confidentiality is of the utmost importance in therapist–client interactions, its importance is somewhat less so within the context of forensic assessment. That is, the nature of forensic evaluation is such that the evaluator is required to provide information about the evaluee, generally in the form of a written report, but also potentially in the form of testimony. However, it is important to recognize that professional guidelines still advise that forensic evaluees be made aware of their rights with respect to confidentiality and that forensic evaluators still maintain confidentiality of information not directly related to the legal purpose of the evaluation.

Section V of the Specialty Guidelines for Forensic Psychologists (Committee on Ethical Guidelines for Forensic Psychologists, 1991) delineates a number of guidelines with respect to confidentiality and privilege (discussed next). Specifically, "Forensic psychologists inform their clients of the limitations to the confidentiality of their services and their products by providing them with an understandable statement of their rights, privileges, and the limitations of confidentiality" (p. 660). In addition,

> In situations where the right of the client or party to confidentiality is limited, the forensic psychologist makes every effort to maintain confidentiality with regard to any information that does not bear directly upon the legal purpose of the evaluation. (p. 660)

Section IV.E. of the American Academy of Psychiatry and the Law (AAPL) Practice Guideline for the Forensic Psychiatric Evaluation of Competence to Stand Trial (Mossman et al., 2007) also delineates that psychiatrists attempt to communicate the lack of confidentiality of the interview and the findings to evaluees.

Thus, it is important that the forensic evaluator provide the relevant information regarding the limits of confidentiality to the defendant being evaluated. Even those exceptions to confidentiality mandated by law, such as elder or child abuse or neglect, should be disclosed to the forensic evaluee. It is important to note, however, that when the evaluator is privately retained by the defense attorney, reporting of legally mandated information to the usual authorities may be inappropriate, given that the evaluator's work is covered under the attorney–client privilege (see next section). In this case, the defense attorney should be made aware of the defendant's disclosure of information requiring legally mandated reporting.

Privilege

Within the context of forensic evaluation, the issue of privilege is essentially irrelevant to communication between the defendant and the examiner. As a court-appointed evaluator, information obtained about the defendant relevant to the legal issue in question is provided to all parties in the form of a written report. Thus, no assertion of privileged communications between the evaluator and the evaluee can be made. When retained by the defense, the *ex parte* evaluator is acting as an agent of the defendant's attorney, and all information obtained during the course of the evaluation becomes part of the attorney's work product. These communications thus become protected by attorney–client privilege (until such time that a report is submitted or testimony offered).

Duty to Protect

Although most jurisdictions recognize a duty to protect, as per *Tarasoff v. Regents of the University of California* (1976), this duty usually applies to situations in which: (1) a patient has communicated a serious threat of physical violence, and (2) this threat is made against a reasonably identifiable victim or victims. It is unclear whether this *Tarasoff*-like duty (which was in the context of a psychotherapist–patient relationship) extends to the evaluator–evaluee relationship; thus, forensic examiners should be familiar with any *Tarasoff*-like statutes in the jurisdictions in which they practice. For those examiners who are functioning as *ex parte* evaluators retained by defense counsel, any specific threats of violence against an identifiable victim should be brought to the attention of the defense attorney. For those examiners who are functioning as court-appointed evaluators, the American Bar Association's Criminal Justice Mental Health Standards (1989) recommend that these types of threats be brought to the attention of the court, as well as the defense attorney. Of course, examiners should be familiar with the relevant jurisdictional requirements regarding the duty to protect and should follow these accordingly.

Informed Consent

Whether informed consent must be obtained before conducting an evaluation of CST depends upon the context of the evaluation. If the evaluation is court-ordered, the defendant generally does not have the right to refuse to participate in the evaluation and thus informed consent need not be obtained. The defendant, however, must be notified regarding the purpose of the evaluation, the limits on confidentiality, the methods to be used in the evaluation, the potential uses of the results of the evaluation, and who will have access to these, as well as the consequences of refusing to participate in the evaluation (detailed information regarding notification is presented in Chapter 5). If, after proper notification, the defendant refuses to participate or cooperate with the assessment, the evaluator must determine whether this is simply a refusal to cooperate or whether the refusal reflects an *inability* to cooperate (due to symptoms of mental disorder) that may be a manifestation of incompetence. In either case, this is important information to note in the report to court.

In the case of an *ex parte* evaluation, the defendant must give informed consent to be evaluated. If, in this type of situation, the defendant refuses to cooperate, the evaluator should put the defendant in touch with her defense counsel.

In general, the same types of information will be provided to obtain informed consent as would be provided in the notification to a defendant who has been court-ordered to undergo a competency evaluation. In the case of obtaining informed consent, however, the evaluator may wish to consider having the defendant sign an informed consent form. In either case (notification or informed consent), the evaluator will want to be sure to document the notification or informed consent procedures in his notes, as well as in the written report.

Multiple Roles

The Specialty Guidelines for Forensic Psychologists discourage forensic psychologists from engaging in multiple relationships, stating,

> Forensic psychologists recognize potential conflicts of interest in dual relationships with parties to a legal proceeding, and they seek to minimize their effects.
>
> 1. Forensic psychologists avoid providing professional services to parties in a legal proceeding with whom they have personal or professional relationships that are inconsistent with the anticipated relationship.
>
> 2. When it is necessary to provide both evaluation and treatment services to a party in a legal proceeding (as may be the case in small forensic hospital settings or small communities), the forensic psychologist takes reasonable steps to minimize

the potential negative effects of these circumstances on the rights of the party, confidentiality, and the process of treatment and evaluation. (Committee on Ethical Guidelines for Forensic Psychologists, 1991, p. 659)

In addition, the AAPL Practice Guideline for the Forensic Psychiatric Evaluation of Competence to Stand Trial also discourages psychiatrists from engaging in conflicting roles with evaluees (Mossman et al., 2007).

Forensic examiners should be clear with evaluees about their role as experts in the case. That is, they serve as evaluators and not as therapists or "helping professionals." In addition, forensic examiners must be careful to maintain their role as objective evaluators and not slip into a therapeutic or helping role with the evaluee.

In addition to being clear about the nature of their role as evaluators, forensic examiners should also make attempts to ensure that they do not fulfill more than one role with an evaluee whenever possible. That is, whenever possible, evaluators should avoid engaging in a therapeutic role with defendants whom they have evaluated. When this is not possible, Melton and colleagues (2007) provide two suggestions. First, "mental health professionals should alert facility administrators to ethical problems related to dual-role assignments and work with them to design services in a way that minimizes this risk" (pp. 86–87). Second, "the clinician should take great care to inform the client/patient of the clinician's dual responsibilities and the limits on confidentiality in therapy imposed by the duty to perform, or inform, collateral forensic evaluations" (p. 87). Furthermore, they recommend that the patient be given periodic reminders of the clinician's dual-role obligation and clarification of the clinician's role in particular sessions.

4
chapter

Privacy

The forensic evaluator should be careful to (1) limit his inquiries to the specific legal issue at hand and (2) not expand the evaluation to include other legal issues. The defendant's right to privacy should be respected

BEST PRACTICE

Elicit only information relevant to the referral question. Do not expand the evaluation to address additional legal issues.

such that the forensic mental health expert should elicit only that information relevant to the referral question. That is, evaluators should be careful not to engage in "voyeurism" in their forensic assessments. With respect to competency evaluations, Melton and colleagues (1997) write, "clinicians who find themselves performing extensive batteries of tests or conducting in-depth psychodynamically oriented interviews routinely in such situations might well explore their motivations for doing so" (p. 91).

Evaluators should be careful not to unilaterally expand the evaluation to address additional legal issues (such as mental state at the time of the offense or risk assessments). Similarly, evaluators cannot use information collected as part of a CST evaluation for the purposes of addressing other legal issues if the defendant was not informed of these additional potential uses of the information obtained. In *Estelle v. Smith* (1981), discussed earlier, the court ruled that clinical information obtained for the purposes of a competency evaluation could not be introduced later at sentencing, since the defendant was not informed that it might be used for the purposes of determining his future dangerousness.

In addition to maintaining a focus on information relevant to the referral question during the course of the assessment, evaluators should also be careful not to violate the defendant's privacy in terms of including sensitive information, irrelevant to the legal issue at hand, in the evaluation report.

Record Keeping

Maintaining Records of All Contacts

Given that the standards of accountability are higher for forensic evaluations than for general clinical assessments, evaluators should be careful to ensure that they are maintaining accurate documentation for each and every step of a forensic evaluation. Detailed written records, including dates and contents, should be kept for every contact made, every conversation held, and every piece of data collected during the course of an evaluation of CST. Psychologist evaluators should be familiar with the American Psychological Association's most recent record keeping guidelines (see APA, 2007).

Information regarding both the process and the content of evaluation methods should be maintained, including the time and sequencing of the various methods used, as well as raw data in the form of interview responses and test item responses. Any psychological testing should be double-checked for accuracy of scoring.

Tracking All Requested Information

The evaluator should maintain a record of all information requested for the assessment, including dates and names of institutions or individuals from whom the information was requested. In addition, records regarding all materials received, including the date and from whom the information was received, should be maintained. Information that was requested but that was not forthcoming should be indicated in the written report.

Challenges to Restoration of Competency

Reevaluation of the issue of competency is required at various intervals (depending upon the statutory requirements of the jurisdiction) for any defendant found incompetent to proceed. Most often, this will take place at the facility where the defendant was sent for competence restoration treatment. As is generally the case, most defendants are restored to competency within a six-month period and returned to court. What, however, is to be done when the defendant's attorney does not believe that the now supposedly restored defendant has attained competence?

This issue was considered by the U.S. District Court in *Duhon v. United States* (2000). The court in *Duhon* rejected the notion that the defendant in this case had been educated into compe-tency through a psychoeducational group (Duhon

4
chapter

> **BEST PRACTICE**
>
> For assessment of restoration to competency, evaluate medication-related issues as well as each of the four prongs:
>
> 1. consult with the lawyer with a reasonable degree of rational understanding,
>
> 2. otherwise assist in the defense,
>
> 3. have a rational understanding of the criminal proceedings, and
>
> 4. have a factual understanding of the proceedings.

was mentally retarded). Further, the court, which posited a four-prong test for competency on the basis of *Dusky* and *Drope*, concluded that the competency reevaluation report submitted for Duhon failed to adequately consider each of these four prongs (specifically, the defendant's ability to consult and "otherwise assist" in his defense). Thus, evaluators must ensure that they are adequately assessing each of the four prongs in both the initial evaluation and subsequent reevaluations of competency.

In addition, since psychotropic medication is the most common form of treatment to "restore" a defendant's competency, evaluators should also ensure that they assess the defendant's compliance with any prescribed medication regime and the role that the medications play in the defendant's competence, as well as the potential impact of the medication (i.e., side effects) or its discontinued use on the defendant's functioning at trial.

The *ex parte* evaluator who has been retained to conduct an independent reevaluation of a defendant's competency after restoration efforts should obtain the initial competency assessment report, records regarding the defendant's competence restoration treatment, and the treating facilities' competency reevaluation report to ensure that all relevant information is evaluated and considered.

Data Collection | 5

—*Data collection should be guided by theories and empirical research findings (within the examiner's areas of expertise) that provide the empirical relations and theoretical assumptions from which causal explanations and predictions generally are made.*

(Grisso, 2003, p. 39)

The purpose of this chapter is to outline and discuss the process of data collection for CST evaluations. Generally, this process can be conceptualized as comprising three different categories of data: information obtained through a clinical interview with the defendant; information obtained through the administration of forensic assessment instruments, forensically relevant, or other psychological tests; and information obtained through collateral or third-party sources. Each of these categories of data will be discussed.

With approximately 60,000 evaluations conducted each year in the United States (Bonnie & Grisso, 2000), CST is the single most common type of criminal forensic assessment. Wide variability exists with respect to the specific demands of each case. Case-specific demands must be a primary consideration in determining what data need be obtained. The quotation at the beginning of this chapter illustrates the importance of using theory and empirical research findings to guide data collection. Just as the contextual demands of each case impact a defendant's competence-related abilities, so too the contextual demands of each case impact the evaluation data to be collected.

Competency evaluations can be performed within a relatively brief timeframe, a fact that can be both

BEST PRACTICE

Collect data depending upon the contextual demands of the case.

encouraging and burdensome (in the case of state employees who are assigned high caseloads with numerous competency evaluations to be conducted). Real-life demands are such that most evaluators are often required to conduct multiple evaluations in a relatively short period and for minimal compensation. The key to managing these demands is an accurate determination regarding the most relevant pieces of data to obtain. At a minimum, the most straightforward (or "typical") case will require an interview with the defendant (targeted specifically at the functional abilities relevant to the context of the proceedings) and the collection of collateral information (regarding the charges/allegations, their possible consequences, and the abilities required of the defendant to proceed). Any additional information to be collected will depend upon the specific nature of the defendant's case and his presenting characteristics.

The Clinical Interview

Preparation for the clinical interview with the defendant can take many forms and is mainly a matter of personal preference; however, at a minimum, the evaluator should have ascertained

- information regarding the charges and allegations that the defendant is facing,

- an explanation regarding what led to the issue of competency being raised (including any specific observations of defense counsel regarding abilities and/or deficits noted), and

- information from the defense attorney regarding the abilities required of the defendant specific to the context of the case.

Given that many competency evaluations require completion within a relatively short timeframe, it is most expedient for the evaluator to have reviewed as much of the available information as possible about the defendant before going into the clinical interview. Obviously, the amount of information available will vary by case; however, the examiner should make

BEST PRACTICE
Review as much available information as possible before the clinical interview.

reasonable attempts to collect as much relevant information as possible. Reviewing the available information ahead of time allows the evaluator to compare the defendant's version of events (both with respect to the competence-related inquiries as well as with respect to the defendant's history) with those from collateral information sources. The evaluator can then confront the defendant regarding any discrepancies during the clinical interview, rather than have to come back an additional time.

Notification

One of the first things that the evaluator should do is provide the defendant with the relevant notification information and obtain informed consent (if necessary). At a minimum, the defendant should be notified regarding

- the purpose of the evaluation,

- for whom the evaluation is being performed (and to whom a report may be submitted),

- the procedures to be used for the evaluation (e.g., interview, third-party data sources, testing) and the types of information to be elicited,

- the possibility that testimony by the examiner in legal proceedings to determine competency may be required,

- the additional limits on confidentiality in terms of those types of information that may require special disclosure to third parties (e.g., legally required child abuse and/or elder abuse reporting), and

- whether the defendant has the right to refuse to participate in the evaluation and the potential consequences of refusal.

A sample notification form can be found in Appendix C.

COURT-ORDERED EVALUATIONS

In many jurisdictions, defendants who have been court-ordered to undergo an evaluation of their CST do not have the right to refuse participation; thus, there is no need to obtain informed consent

5
chapter

from the defendant for court-ordered evaluations. In these cases, the defendant should be provided with the relevant notification information, engaged by the evaluator in a dialogue about the information presented, and asked to sign a copy of the notification form or indicate his understanding of the notification orally. The evaluator should be sure to give the defendant an opportunity to ask questions, which should be answered in a candid manner. A signed copy (or a copy with a notation by the evaluator that the defendant indicated his understanding orally) of the notification should be kept in the evaluator's file and a copy of the notification can be provided to the defendant to keep.

EX PARTE EVALUATIONS

In defense-requested *ex parte* evaluations, informed consent should be obtained from the defendant before proceeding with the evaluation. All relevant notification information should be provided to the defendant, and the evaluator should engage the defendant in a dialogue about the information presented to ensure an adequate understanding on the part of the defendant. Once the evaluator is satisfied that the defendant understands the relevant information, informed consent should be obtained. A signed copy (or a copy with a notification indicating that the defendant gave informed consent orally) of the informed consent form should be retained in the evaluator's file and a copy given to the defendant to keep. If the evaluator has reason to suspect that the defendant is unable to give informed consent, he should contact the retaining attorney to discuss this issue and to obtain informed consent on the client's behalf (this may be from the defendant's attorney or from a responsible family member). In these cases, the assent of the defendant should be obtained in addition to informed consent from a responsible party.

Background and History

The amount of background and historical information collected for any defendant depends, to some extent, on the context and circumstances of the case, as well as the characteristics of the defendant. Several different domains or types of background or historical information can be collected, including early family history, educational history, marital history (including whether the defendant has any children), military history, religious history, employment history, alcohol and drug use history, sexual history (for sexual offenses), history of suicidal or self-injurious behavior, medical history (including whether the defendant has suffered any major injuries or suffers from any diseases), legal history, and psychiatric history (including history of treatment). The amount of information collected in each of these domains will depend upon the circumstances of the case and the characteristics of the defendant. For example, more information will be elicited about prior mental health treatment and psychiatric hospitalization for a defendant with a history of mental illness than for a defendant with no history of mental illness. Similarly, more information about a defendant's drug and alcohol use will be elicited from a defendant whose defense attorney believes that substance use is impairing that defendant's performance than from a defendant who strictly adheres to religious prohibitions against the use of drugs or alcohol.

Some forensic mental health professionals believe that the focus of CST evaluations should remain solely on the defendant's present functioning and, therefore, argue that no historical information need be obtained. We disagree with this perspective for two reasons. First, we believe that context is always important; thus, it is only within the context of an individual's previous functioning (history or background) that we can fully understand and interpret her current level of functioning. Second, it is often difficult, if not impossible, to know what factors will eventually turn out to be important or pivotal for a case; thus, it appears important to have at least some knowledge regarding the defendant's background in each of the relevant domains. For these two reasons, it is important to conduct an interview with the defendant to inquire about each of the relevant domains. As indicated earlier, the amount of detail to be covered within each domain may be tailored to the context of the case and the characteristics of the defendant. Those domains that appear to be irrelevant to either the context of the case or the characteristics of the defendant can either be eliminated from inquiry or significantly limited, whereas

BEST PRACTICE
Gather historical information in the domains relevant to the defendant's case.

those domains that appear to be of particular relevance can become subject to more detailed inquiry.

Questions about a defendant's background and history are often an easy means of establishing rapport, as these types of questions are generally less threatening to the defendant. The evaluator can begin with these types of questions and eventually work her way toward asking questions that are generally perceived as more threatening to the defendant, such as those regarding the current charge(s) that the defendant is facing, the circumstances surrounding those charges and allegations, and possible sentences that might be imposed if found guilty. Thus, in addition to allowing the evaluator an opportunity to develop a sense of the current functioning of the defendant within the context of his previous functioning, the evaluator is also able to develop rapport with the defendant by inquiring about his background and history.

Two additional benefits are obtained by conducting an inquiry into the defendant's background and history. First, it allows the evaluator to collect a sample of the defendant's verbal behavior and to draw inferences about the defendant's thought content and organization. Since this is done within the context of relatively nonthreatening questions, the defendant is more likely to feel at ease. Thus, the evaluator will then be able to compare the defendant's verbal behavior (and related inferences regarding thought content and organization) in this context with her verbal behavior within a more threatening context, such as when being asked questions pertaining to her mental health and functioning or her current criminal charges. Second, it allows the evaluator to obtain information from the defendant that can be verified through third-party information sources, thus providing the opportunity for a reliability check.

Current Clinical Assessment

The current clinical functioning of the defendant is at issue in a competency evaluation; thus, a current clinical assessment, including a mental status examination and diagnostic inquiries, is a necessary component of the clinical interview with the defendant. In the next chapter, we will discuss, in detail, the issue of determining or establishing the linkage between psychiatric symptoms and deficits in competence-related abilities. The first step in attempting to determine or establish this linkage is in developing a comprehensive understanding and assessment of the defendant's current clinical functioning. To do this, the evaluator will need to ask questions and make observations of the defendant in a number of different clinical domains. These include, but are not limited to the following:

- general appearance and attitude (including observations regarding dress and grooming; personal hygiene; marks, scars, or other notable observations; and general attitude and demeanor);

- cognitive functioning (including memory; orientation; concentration and attention; fund of information; abstract reasoning ability; judgment and insight; estimated intelligence; speech productivity, flow, tone, and understandability; thought productivity and structure; hallucinations; and delusions or other unusual content);

- motor activity, eye contact, mannerisms, use of gestures, facial expressions, quality of mood, range of affect, and affective control.

In addition, for those defendants who are on psychotropic medication at the time of the evaluation, the evaluator will need to assess the defendant's compliance with the prescribed medication regime. The evaluator must also consider the potential impact that the medication (i.e., side effects) might have on the defendant's functioning during the proceedings.

The structure and format of the inquiries necessary to make a comprehensive current clinical assessment of the defendant will vary according to the preferences of the individual evaluator. It should be noted that, historically, an emphasis was placed on diagnosis in competency evaluation, with certain diagnoses, such as

BEST PRACTICE

When assessing a defendant's current clinical functioning, be sure to note specific symptoms.

5
chapter

psychosis, being equated with incompetence (see Chapter 3); however, over time, the emphasis on diagnosis has diminished, whereas the emphasis on legal functioning has increased. Thus, it is not diagnosis *per se* that is important in determining whether a defendant is impaired in terms of his competence-related abilities. Rather, it is the presence of symptoms that interfere with or impair a defendant's functioning in one or more competence-related abilities that is of interest. That is, a symptom-level focus may be more relevant to competency evaluation than simply a determination of diagnosis (see Chapter 2 for a discussion of functional assessments). Therefore, a comprehensive clinical assessment should take into consideration a defendant's cognitive and psychiatric functioning, as well as the presence of specific symptoms. This will set a solid foundation for determining whether there is a linkage to any observed deficits in competence-related (psycholegal) abilities.

Issues Specific to Competency

In addition to inquiries about the defendant's background and history and an assessment of the defendant's current clinical functioning, the evaluator must also inquire about issues specific to CST. It is generally easiest to make these inquiries after having developed a rapport or working relationship with the defendant (e.g., after collecting information on the defendant's history and background). The structure and format of competence-related inquiries will depend upon the personal preferences of the evaluator; however, a competency-specific forensic assessment instrument, such as the Fitness Interview Test–Revised (FIT-R) or the Interdisciplinary Fitness Interview–Revised (IFI-R) may be useful to structure this portion of the interview. Other forensic assessment instruments, such as the MacArthur Competence Assessment Tool–Criminal Adjudication (MacCAT-CA) or the Evaluation of Competency to Stand Trial–Revised (ECST-R), may be useful to administer as a means of determining how the defendant compares (normatively) with other defendants in terms of specific competence-related abilities.

As discussed previously, the evaluator should be familiar with and knowledgeable about the relevant criteria for competence in her jurisdiction, since many of the specific inquiries will flow directly from these criteria. In addition to general inquiries regarding the nature, object, and consequences of the court proceedings, the forensic mental health professional will also want to ask the defendant questions about why he was referred for a competency evaluation (obviously, the information the evaluator received regarding the reason for the referral will be invaluable here) as well as inquiries about the defendant's relationship with counsel.

In addition to being knowledgeable about the specific jurisdictional criteria for competency, the evaluator should also have a general familiarity with the literature on CST. A number of competence-related abilities have been identified in the available literature on competency, and the evaluator should be careful to consider each of these abilities in relation to the specific context of the defendant's case and the specific characteristics of the defendant. Even if the jurisdictional criteria for competence do not use the same words as the literature, the evaluator should be knowledgeable about the ways in which the competence criteria have been interpreted and used in case law within the jurisdiction. It is quite possible that a jurisdiction may use a term such as "understand the personal importance of" or "rational understanding" rather than the word "appreciate," but the knowledgeable evaluator will understand that the same ability is being referred to by both of these terms.

Finally, it is important for evaluators to recognize the distinction between *capacity* and *ability*. If a defendant is unable to provide a particular piece of information, it should not be assumed that his inability to do so reflects incapacity. Rather, the evaluator should attempt to tease apart capacity from ability by disclosing the relevant information to the defendant and then making inquiries about the disclosed information at a later point in the evaluation.

BEST PRACTICE

Assess the defendant with respect to each of the various competence-related abilities that have been identified in the literature and apply them to the case as appropriate, including

- understanding,
- appreciation,
- reasoning,
- decision making,
- communicating or consulting with counsel, and
- assisting in his or her defense.

BEWARE
Don't assume inability equals incapacity.

FORENSIC ASSESSMENT INSTRUMENTS

One forensic assessment instrument, the MacCAT-CA, was developed to assist in the evaluation of CST by providing a means of comparing a particular defendant's performance on three competence-related abilities—understanding, reasoning, and appreciation—to the typical (normative) performance of defendants. Although the MacCAT-CA (as well as any other forensic assessment instrument) represents only one component of the competency evaluation (i.e., supplies only one piece of relevant data), having some indication of where a particular defendant falls in terms of his abilities relative to other defendants is a potentially useful piece of information.

Other forensic assessment instruments, such as the FIT-R or the IFI-R, were developed as a means of guiding the evaluator through many of the relevant areas of inquiry specific to CST. Of course, the context and circumstances of the case and the particular characteristics of the defendant may necessitate additional areas of inquiry; however, the FIT-R captures the majority of the relevant areas for the majority of cases. The IFI-R also leads the evaluator through many of the various relevant areas of inquiry. (See Appendix D for a list of relevant competence-related domains and suggested areas of inquiry.)

HANDLING INCRIMINATING INFORMATION

Since evaluators must ask about the defendant's current charges and her understanding of the allegations surrounding those charges as part of any competency evaluation, it is important to remember that, although relevant to the assessment of a defendant's competency, this information also has the potential to be incriminating for the defendant. How is an evaluator to handle this situation? Whereas some commentators have recommended that the evaluator not ask the defendant any questions specifically about the index offense(s), it appears to us that this tactic is problematic in that it does not allow the evaluator to make an assessment regarding whether the defendant is able to provide relevant information to his defense counsel. Since we promote a functional evaluation of competency, we believe that it is impossible to evaluate all relevant aspects of a defendant's competence-related abilities without asking specifically about the index offense(s). As addressed in Chapter 7, evaluators must be cautious about what they write in their reports and ensure that general statements about the "process" rather than specific statements about the "content" of the defendant's account are used. If the evaluator is careful to avoid including incriminating information in the report, there is no reason to skirt the issue of asking the defendant specific questions about the index offense(s).

BEST PRACTICE

Ask specifically about the index offense(s) during the clinical interview, but be aware that self-incriminating information should not be included in the report.

Trial Demands

An assessment of an individual's competency entails an evaluation of the degree of congruence or incongruence between the individual's functional abilities and the specific situational demands of her case. Therefore, it is important for the evaluator to have a clear understanding of the potential abilities required of each defendant, as well as the situational demands of the case. Grisso (2003, pp. 87–88) compiled a list of variables or factors that might be gathered to assist in evaluating the defendant's ability to meet specific trial demands. This list includes the

- complexity and multiplicity of charges;
- particular events associated with the alleged offense;
- range of possible penalties for this alleged offense, and probabilities of their occurrence;
- range and types of evidence available to counsel without defendant's report;
- simplicity or complexity of the legal defenses available;
- necessity for defendant's own testimony at trial;
- probable length of trial;
- probable complexity of trial (e.g., types and numbers of witnesses);
- potential of trial to arouse emotion (e.g., due to the nature of the offense, relation of parties in the trial process); and

5
chapter

- sources of social support for defendant during trial process.

Once the evaluator has determined the particular abilities required of the defendant for the specific legal proceedings, these factors can be used to guide the competence-related inquiries.

Observed Interactions With Defense Counsel

A functional approach to the evaluation of a defendant's CST is based on the notion that the defendant who is able to perform specific competence-related actions or tasks during the course of the evaluation should be able to perform those same actions or tasks when working with his defense attorney or at trial. Similarly, the defendant who is unable to perform some competence-related task during the course of the evaluation is also unlikely to be able to perform that task at trial or when working with his defense attorney (unless, perhaps, interventions designed to increase the likelihood of the defendant being able to perform the task are employed). A functional evaluation, then, requires that the defendant be given the opportunity to perform competence-relevant tasks, so that the evaluator can then extrapolate from the defendant's performance during the evaluation and form an opinion about his abilities within the context of the criminal proceedings he faces.

Grisso (2003) noted that the most fundamental objective of a competency assessment is to "obtain information about a person's functional abilities—*what the person understands, knows, believes, or can do that is directly related to the competence construct*" (p. 25, italics in original). Further, Grisso states, "*Whenever possible, therefore, forensic examiners should observe directly the functional abilities associated with a legal competence*" (p. 26, italics in original). The interaction between the defendant and defense counsel is an important consideration in any competency evaluation and thus, whenever possible, this interaction should be directly observed. Direct observation will allow the evaluator to make an informed judgment about the ability of the defendant to work with her defense attorney. In addition, direct observation may allow for potential remediation of any noted problems or deficiencies in the interaction between the defendant and her defense attorney.

The evaluator may choose to "prepare" the defense attorney with a list of questions or information to work through with the defendant during observation by the evaluator; it is often the case that this preparation

BEST PRACTICE
When possible, directly observe the interaction between the defendant and the defense attorney to assess performance of competence-related tasks.

allows the expert to observe legally relevant interaction between the defense attorney and the defendant. Useful content areas to observe include having the defense attorney review possible legal defenses with the defendant, engaging the defendant in a discussion of possible legal strategies to be used, and eliciting information from the defendant regarding her version of the alleged events.

Of course, some of what is said between attorney and client regarding the facts of the case may well be privileged and should not be included in the report. Only those statements that capture the process of the interactions, rather than the specific content, should be included in the report.

It may be that logistic constraints do not allow the evaluator to observe the interaction between the defendant and the defense attorney. In this case, the evaluator will have to extrapolate from his own interactions with the defendant the manner in which she should be able to interact with defense counsel. In addition, the defendant's observations, attitudes, and reported experiences with the defense attorney will need to be taken into consideration by the evaluator.

Issues of Response Style

A defendant's response style must be considered in any forensic evaluation. In cases in which the defendant appears to be responding in any way other than candid, honest, or straightforward, a formal evaluation of response style (incorporating data from interview, testing, and third-party information sources) is warranted. Thus, the collection of relevant third-party and collateral information becomes of primary importance as a means of confirming the defendant's self-report and evaluating his response style in any forensic evaluation. Different types of response styles exist (e.g., malingering, defensive, irrelevant, random, honest, and hybrid, as delineated by Rogers,

1997; reliable/honest, malingering, defensive, and irrelevant, as delineated by Heilbrun, 2001), but one—malingering (feigned response style)—must always be considered by any evaluator working within the forensic context. With respect to this issue, Melton and colleagues (2007) recommend that forensic evaluators have a "low threshold for suspecting dissimulation . . . accompanied by a conservative stance with respect to reaching conclusions on that issue" (p. 57).

The evaluation of a defendant's response style can be made on the basis of interviewing techniques and observation, formal testing, and a comparison of self-report information with that obtained from third-party and collateral information sources. We recommend that evaluators obtain data from third-party/collateral information sources and directly from the defendant in every case, then use testing to collect additional data for those cases that appear to warrant further evaluation. Testing may include the use of both forensically relevant instruments (such as the Structured Interview of Reported Symptoms [SIRS; Rogers, Bagby, & Dickens, 1992], the Validity Indicator Profile [VIP; Frederick, 1997], or the Test of Memory Malingering [TOMM; Tombaugh, 1996]) and/or psychological instruments (such as the Minnesota Multiphasic Personality Inventory–2 [MMPI-2; Hathaway & McKinley, 1989]; see later section in this chapter). It is difficult to underestimate the utility of confronting the defendant with respect to inconsistencies between his self-report and information obtained through third-party and collateral sources in the evaluation of response style.

One final word with respect to malingering; it is important for the evaluator to remember that a defendant may malinger in two different ways relevant to CST—feigning or exaggerating mental illness/psychiatric symptomatology and feigning or exaggerating mental impairment/cognitive deficit. Therefore, the evaluator must consider the totality of the defendant's responses in all relevant areas. Once a conclusion regarding the defendant's response style has been reached, the evaluator must be sure to weigh information obtained through the defendant's self-report accordingly.

Special Issues With Various Examinee Populations
INDIVIDUALS WITH MENTAL RETARDATION (INTELLECTUAL DISABILITY)

Research and commentary on the competency of individuals with mental retardation has highlighted a number of important issues. Scholars such as Bonnie (1992a) have noted that this population tends to be under-identified. That is, a considerable number of individuals with mental retardation are not referred for psychological evaluations. Bonnie hypothesized that this low rate of referral is due to a general failure to recognize the magnitude and/or existence of the disabilities of those with mental retardation.

Persons with mental retardation often attempt to hide their limitations by acting in a compliant and cooperative way with authority figures, and often pretend to understand their lawyers when they, in fact, may not (Bonnie, 1992a). This "cloak of competence" (Edgerton, 1993) gives these individuals an appearance of normalcy; thus, legally significant impairments become visible only when the individual has a mental illness or acts in a strange or disruptive manner. It is common for these individuals to proceed to trial without ever having been identified or evaluated with respect to their competence to proceed (Cooper & Grisso, 1997).

Simply having mental retardation does not make an individual incompetent to proceed; however, available research appears to demonstrate a higher probability of being found incompetent for individuals with mental retardation as compared to those without (see Ericson & Perlman, 2001; Everington & Dunn, 1995). The defendant must be evaluated with respect to her competence-related abilities to determine whether any competence-related impairments exist. Thus, it is important that these individuals are evaluated by an expert familiar with the specific issues relevant to mental retardation.

Qualified evaluators should be aware that there exists a forensic assessment

BEST PRACTICE

For referrals of individuals with mental retardation, be certain that you possess the relevant knowledge and experience to conduct competency assessments with this population. If this is not the case, the referral should be transferred to an evaluator who has expertise in this area.

instrument developed specifically for the purpose of assisting in the evaluation of CST in individuals with mental retardation (see Chapter 3)—the Competence Assessment for Standing Trial for Defendants with Mental Retardation (CAST*MR; Everington & Luckasson, 1992). As is the case with any other competence-specific forensic assessment instrument, the results of the CAST*MR constitute one piece of data to be incorporated within the larger context of the competency evaluation.

Specific techniques that have been recommended for use in the evaluation of individuals with mental retardation include

- using open-ended questions (as opposed to yes/no questions),

- using language appropriate to the developmental level or level of understanding of the individual,

- using confrontational questioning to assess the ability to withstand cross-examination,

- observing the defendant in consultation with her attorney to gain a sense of her strengths and weaknesses,

- providing simple definitions or explanations of legal concepts, and

- asking questions to ensure that the defendant understands any information presented and is not merely parroting back or acquiescing (see Appelbaum, 1994; Ericson & Perlman, 2001).

Rates of incompetence among individuals with mental retardation vary widely but, as a general statement, a relationship appears to exist between degree of mental retardation and the probability of being considered incompetent, with those individuals having moderate mental retardation being found incompetent at higher rates than those with mild mental retardation (Petrella, 1992). In terms of the restoration of competency in individuals with mental retardation, a recent analysis of the predictors of restorability indicate that the presence of mental retardation was associated with a lower probability of restoration (Mossman, 2007).

INDIVIDUALS WITH ACUTE PSYCHOSIS OR OTHER
SEVERE MENTAL ILLNESS

The issue of what to do with those individuals who are acutely psychotic at the time of evaluation or who are displaying other signs of severe mental illness that significantly impairs their day-to-day functioning most often hinges on the current living situation of the defendant. For those defendants housed at a forensic facility, the evaluator can speak with the attending physician to determine whether the defendant can be medicated or treated in such a way as to reduce the symptoms of the psychosis or other severe mental disorder before proceeding with the evaluation. For those defendants being held at a jail or other pre-trial facility, the evaluator can speak with the facility medical staff to determine the feasibility of medication or other treatment for the defendant before proceeding with the evaluation. In those cases in which it is not possible, because of institutional or statutory procedure, to administer medication or other treatment to reduce the defendant's severe symptoms, the evaluator may wish to proceed with the evaluation, making clear the defendant's lack of ability to give meaningful assent to the evaluation in the evaluation report.

In those cases in which the evaluator is retained directly by the defense counsel to perform an *ex parte* evaluation, and thus has an obligation to obtain informed consent from the defendant or the defendant's guardian before proceeding, the evaluator should contact the retaining attorney to determine how best to proceed. In those (rare) instances in which the defendant is not in an inpatient facility but rather is living in the community, the expert should inform the referring party about the acute state of the defendant. It is possible that instigation of civil commitment proceedings may be necessary for those individuals whose acute mental state is causing them to become dangerous to themselves or others and thus meet criteria for commitment. Alternatively, it may be the case that a court-ordered competency evaluation to be conducted at an inpatient facility could be requested.

In those cases in which the evaluator is able to proceed with the competency assessment, Goldstein and Burd (1990) noted that various factors must be considered including the likelihood of

5
chapter

deterioration in the defendant's mental state before adjudication of his case, possible signs of deterioration, and factors that are likely to precipitate deterioration. In addition, these authors highlight the need for the evaluator to inquire about the defendant's background, education, literacy, prior legal (court) experience, and psychiatric treatment history in making a determination regarding his competence-related abilities.

For any defendant being treated with psychotropic medication at the time of the assessment, the evaluator must consider the effects of the medication on the defendant's functional abilities (e.g., capacity to track the proceedings given the sedative effect of the medication). The evaluator's report should include information regarding relevant issues, such as the potentially detrimental effects of the medication on the defendant's courtroom demeanor.

INDIVIDUALS WITH AMNESIA

Cases in which the defendant is claiming to have amnesia for the time of the alleged crime may require the evaluator to make a determination regarding the veracity of the claim. Sources of third-party or collateral information should be sought by the evaluator in an attempt to corroborate the claim of amnesia. In addition, the evaluator should inform the defendant that having amnesia for the time of the crime would not necessarily lead to a finding of incompetence; this, by itself, may cause the defendant to suddenly "recover" the relevant memories.

As discussed in Chapter 1, the issue of amnesia as it relates to CST has been considered by the courts, and a unanimous refusal to equate amnesia with incompetence has emerged. The court in *Wilson* (1968) delineated six guidelines (see Chapter 1) to assist in determining whether an amnesic defendant was competent. Thus, the court adopted a functional approach, wherein the evaluation of competency is based on a determination of the manner in which a defendant's incapacity might have an effect on the legal proceedings. The evaluator, therefore, should examine each of the six *Wilson* criteria, as well as any others that appear to be pertinent to the case, to ensure that a thorough analysis of the potential impact of the amnesia has been made.

INDIVIDUALS POSING A THREAT TO THE EXAMINER

In those rare instances in which the defendant poses a threat to the evaluator, it may be necessary to take precautionary measures to ensure the evaluator's safety. For defendants assessed at a jail or inpatient facility, the expert can request that a correctional officer or security guard be assigned to stand outside the evaluation room door (or inside the evaluation room if absolutely necessary). Although it is certainly not optimal for developing rapport, the evaluator may also request that the defendant be shackled or hand-cuffed during the evaluation. If the evaluation is to be conducted on an outpatient basis, some states allow court-ordered evaluators the opportunity to see defendants at a state forensic facility where security officers can be assigned to assist if necessary. If the evaluator has been retained to conduct an *ex parte* evaluation, and the defendant poses a real and significant threat to the evaluator's safety, she may insist that the defense attorney be present during the evaluation. (If the defense attorney is not willing to be present, the evaluator may consider giving up any income that the evaluation might bring and simply refuse the case!)

JUVENILES

The evaluation of juvenile trial competence is a burgeoning field that is not covered in this volume. The interested reader is referred to *Evaluations of Juveniles' Competence to Stand Trial* by Kruh and Grisso (2009), another volume in this series, for detailed information regarding best practices in assessing trial competence of juveniles.

Testing

Forensic Assessment Instruments

Grisso (2003) outlined a number of advantages, both conceptual and procedural, of using forensic assessment instruments (FAIs). Conceptually, forensic assessment instruments provide structure for the examiner, help to improve communication in legal settings, and facilitate empirical research on the associations between psychological constructs and legally relevant functional abilities. Procedurally, the benefits of forensic assessment instruments and the standardization of the assessment process that they promote include reduction of error and bias, the promotion of meaningful comparisons across time, allowing for the collection of data on normative samples, the facilitation of comparisons between examiners, and the possibility of programs of research on the empirical reliability of examiners' methods and the validity of their assessment data (pp. 46–47).

To summarize, Grisso (2003) stated,

> FAIs [forensic assessment instruments] provide operational definitions for functional abilities that are related conceptually to legal competence constructs as well as our psychological and psychiatric constructs. Therefore, they offer two main potential benefits. One is to assist examiners in constructing assessments with conceptual relevance to legal criteria. The other is to contribute data to forensic assessments in a manner consistent with scientific standards for the reliability and validity of assessments. (p. 47)

Thus, those forensic examiners who do not use FAIs to assist in their evaluations of CST are encouraged to consider the utility of these instruments for their practice in this area.

SELECTING AN APPROPRIATE FORENSIC ASSESSMENT INSTRUMENT

Numerous FAIs exist for the assessment of CST (see Chapter 3 for a review of these FAIs). Some of these, such as the IFI-R and the FIT-R, were developed to guide the evaluator through many of the topic areas relevant to CST. Others, such as the ECST-R and the MacCAT-CA, were developed to assist evaluators in assessing various relevant psycholegal domains in a way that allows for normative comparisons of defendants. In addition, other instruments, such as the CAST*MR, were developed for use with specific populations of defendants. Strengths and limitations are associated with each forensic assessment instrument, and it is up to the evaluator to select an instrument that will work well with his personal style, as well as with the specific needs of the defendant to be evaluated.

Numerous case- and defendant-specific factors must be considered when selecting an appropriate forensic assessment instrument, including but not limited to

- the seriousness of the charges,
- whether a plea has been offered,
- whether the defendant will be required to testify,
- whether or not there is a feasible defense,
- whether the defendant has a developmental disability,
- and whether the characteristics of the defendant's case are such that the defendant will be required to provide all relevant information to defense counsel (as opposed to those cases in which additional sources of information, other than the defendant, are available).

The forensic evaluator should become familiar with the strengths and limitations of the various forensic assessment instruments developed to assist in the evaluation of CST and should consider these carefully when selecting an instrument to use in a particular case. To gain the benefit of consistency, as well as the ability to make comparisons across time and defendants, we recommend that each evaluator select a forensic assessment instrument that can be used in the majority of his cases and then to supplement the data supplied by this forensic assessment instrument with data from other FAIs as necessary.

Forensically Relevant Instruments

Forensically relevant instruments are those that assist in evaluating characteristics or conditions that, although not the specific focus of legal inquiry, are relevant to evaluations of specific legal inquiries. Two of the most important of these conditions or characteristics that must be considered in any forensic evaluation are malingering and psychopathy. Thus, forensically relevant instruments are those that focus on the evaluation of malingering or psychopathy as a means of assisting the evaluator

5
chapter

BEST PRACTICE
Become familiar with the strengths and limitations of any forensically relevant instrument before selecting it for use in a forensic evaluation.

in forming an opinion regarding a relevant area of legal inquiry, such as CST. As is the case with FAIs, forensically relevant instruments each have their strengths and limitations.

MALINGERING

Malingering, the feigned production or exaggeration of psychological, cognitive, or physical symptoms to achieve some external incentive, must be ruled out in every legal context, including CST. Several forensically relevant instruments have been developed to assist in the evaluation of malingering. Instruments such as the Structured Interview of Reported Symptoms (SIRS; Rogers, Bagby, & Dickens, 1992) and the Miller Forensic Assessment of Symptoms Test (M-FAST; Miller, 1995) were developed to assist in the evaluation of malingering of psychiatric impairment, whereas instruments such as the Validity Indicator Profile (VIP; Frederick, 1997) and the Test of Memory Malingering (TOMM; Tombaugh, 1996) were developed to assist in the assessment of malingering of cognitive impairment. In addition, the aforementioned ECST-R (Rogers, Tillbrook, & Sewell, 2004) is a competency assessment instrument that includes a scale for the evaluation of feigned incompetence.

PSYCHOPATHY

Psychopathy, a constellation of affective, interpersonal, and behavioral characteristics, may arise as a clinical issue in the full range of criminal forensic assessments, including CST. Although a direct link between psychopathy and competency status has yet to be explored, some evidence suggests that individuals high on the trait of psychopathy are more likely to attempt to malinger or feign mental disorder or incompetence (Ciccone, 2007; Gacono, Meloy, Sheppard, Speth, & Roske, 1995; Heinze & Vess, 2005). Instruments such as the Hare Psychopathy Checklist–Revised (PCL-R; Hare, 1991, 2003) and the Hare Psychopathy Checklist: Screening Version (PCL:SV; Hart, Cox, & Hare, 1995) were developed to assist in the evaluation of psychopathy using file review and an interview with the defendant, whereas instruments such as the Psychopathic Personality Inventory (PPI; Lilienfeld & Andrews, 1996) use a self-report rating format.

Psychological Testing
DETERMINING THE NECESSITY FOR PSYCHOLOGICAL TESTING

In every case, the evaluator will need to determine whether there is a need for psychological testing. In some cases, psychological testing is warranted to provide further information about a specific, relevant characteristic or condition. For example, intelligence testing may be appropriate and necessary in those cases in which the intellectual ability of the defendant is at issue or when the examiner is unsure about whether the defendant meets criteria for having mental retardation or another developmental disability. In this situation, psychological testing may be necessary to assist the examiner in determining where the defendant falls in terms of her intellectual and/or adaptive functioning. Similarly, neuropsychological testing may be appropriate in a case in which the defendant appears to be suffering from some form of cognitive deficit and does not appear to be malingering.

SELECTING APPROPRIATE PSYCHOLOGICAL TESTS

In selecting the appropriate psychological tests to administer in those cases that appear to warrant such testing, the evaluator must attend to the issue of relevant evaluee characteristics. That is, tests should be chosen according to the particular issue to be examined, as well as the characteristics of the defendant to be tested. The population upon which the psychological test was validated must be taken into consideration and, as much as possible, should match the characteristics of the population from which the defendant belongs. Defendant characteristics such as age, ethnicity, gender, and presence of disabilities, among others, should be considered.

The goal of psychological testing should always be to gain more data regarding a specific issue under consideration. Of course, it should follow that the specific issue under consideration should have a clear, identifiable link to the relevant legal issue of CST and should address a causal connection to a deficit in one or more of the functional abilities related to CST. Grisso (2003) noted "psychological

BEST PRACTICE

Determine those situations in which there appears to be a need for psychological testing and then choose testing instruments according to the relevant circumstances.

characteristics that may be relevant for developing such causal connections include general intelligence, memory, contact with reality, motivation, reasoning or problem solving, and emotional control" (p. 86).

Collateral Information

Records: Minimal Requirements Versus Aspirational

As has been stated numerous times throughout this book, minimal requirements in terms of collateral information for CST evaluations include information regarding the charges and allegations surrounding those charges, information relevant to the reasons for the referral, and information related to what is to be expected of the defendant in moving forward with his case. In addition, it is often helpful to have some information regarding the defendant's prior criminal history and contacts with the legal system. Of course, a large gray area exists between minimal collateral information requirements and aspirational standards for collateral information. In the perfect world, it would be easy for an evaluator to obtain any and all relevant information about a defendant to inform a competency evaluation; however, it is often the case that evaluators have a relatively short timeframe for completion of an evaluation, and collateral information and records, once identified, are not often quickly forthcoming. It is up to the evaluator to decide which pieces of information are imperative to the assessment (and thus must be obtained before moving forward with the evaluation) and which are merely supplementary. As always, this will depend upon the circumstances of the case and the characteristics of the defendant.

Interviews With Collateral Sources

It is often helpful for the evaluator to speak with other professionals or individuals with whom the defendant has had contact to obtain additional information beyond that given by the defendant. Other mental health professionals who have had contact with the defendant are often able to speak to their impressions of the defendant, as well as about her response to any treatment that has been administered. Jail personnel, both correctional officers as well as mental health or medical staff, are often able to give their impressions of the defendant's functioning. Given that CST focuses on the defendant's current mental state, any person with whom the defendant has had recent contact may be useful to the evaluation.

BEST PRACTICE

Corroborate self-report information from the defendant through third-party or collateral information sources.

Evaluating the Reliability of Collateral Information

Any collateral or third-party information that is obtained as part of a competency evaluation must be evaluated with respect to its accuracy and reliability. It is often assumed that medical or other records are accurate and reliable; however, there may be instances in which the information contained in these records is inaccurate or unreliable. In addition, interviews with third-party sources may not necessarily provide accurate or reliable information. Therefore, it is up to the evaluator to consider all information in light of the source from which it was obtained, to make a determination regarding the veracity of the information, and to weigh the information accordingly in making a judgment about the defendant's CST. Just as evaluators may look to collateral information sources to corroborate information obtained through the defendant's self-report, so too may evaluators look to collateral or third-party information sources to corroborate other sources of information. As a general rule, self-reported information from the defendant should be corroborated through third-party or collateral information sources. (More detailed information on the use of third-party information in forensic assessment can be found in Heilbrun, Warren, & Picarello, 2003 and Otto, Slobogin, & Greenberg, 2007).

5
chapter

Interpretation 6

—*For clinical information to be relevant in addressing legal questions of competence,* examiners must present the logic that links these observations to the specific abilities and capacities with which the law is concerned.

(Grisso, 2003, p. 13, emphasis in original)

The Functional/Contextual Nature of the Evaluation

Throughout this book the functional and contextual nature of competency assessment have been highlighted. The importance of these two concepts cannot be understated. Thus, after collecting all the various pieces of data (e.g., interview data, collateral information, psychological test data), the evaluator must then interpret these data in light of the functional abilities of the defendant and the context of the defendant's case. In the words of Grisso (2003),

> a decision about legal competence is in part a statement about *congruency or incongruency between (a) the extent of a person's functional ability and (b) the degree of performance demand that is made by the specific instance of the context in that case.* Thus, an interaction between individual ability and situational demand, not an absolute level of ability, is of special significance for legal competence decisions. (pp. 32–33, italics in original)

The evaluator's task is to describe the defendant's functional abilities or, as Grisso (2003) states, "to describe as clearly and accurately as possible that which the defendant knows, understands, believes, or can do" (p. 38). There is no absolute cutoff that can be used to determine whether a defendant is able to perform some specific action or task relevant to the legal proceedings; rather, the

BEST PRACTICE
Describe the defendant's functional abilities and deficits within the context of the specific demands of the case.

level of ability demonstrated by the defendant must be considered and described in light of the demands of the defendant's specific case.

To make a determination regarding the degree of congruence or incongruence between the defendant's abilities and the demands of the case, the evaluator must have a good understanding of what will be required of the defendant during the course of the legal proceedings. This information should be obtained through discussions or written communications with the defense attorney. The evaluator should consider all possible relevant trial and non–trial related abilities or demands specific to the defendant's case in describing the defendant's abilities and deficits. Given that competency is an open-textured construct for which no fixed set of abilities can be defined, the evaluator is wise to err on the side of describing the defendant's abilities and deficits on *any* foreseeable case demands when information regarding the specific demands of the defendant's case is uncertain or not forthcoming.

Mental Disorder

The available statutes and guidelines regarding competency either imply or explicitly require that any noted deficits be the result of mental disorder or cognitive disability. Therefore, "the presence of cognitive disability or mental disorder is merely a threshold issue that must be established to 'get one's foot in the competency door'" (Zapf, Skeem, & Golding, 2005, p. 433).

Ascertaining Whether the Defendant Has a Mental Disorder

Determining whether a defendant meets criteria for a mental disorder or cognitive disability is perhaps the area of greatest strength or skill for mental health professionals in their role as forensic evaluators. Each evaluator will have his own preferences for how this is done. What is important to discuss here, however, is that the presence of mental disorder is a separate consideration from the presence of psycholegal deficits. The presence of mental disorder or cognitive disability is a prerequisite to being found incompetent; however, empirical investigations have confirmed that mental disorder exists in individuals who demon-

BEWARE
Presence of either a mental disorder or cognitive disability in itself does not establish incompetency.

strate no functional deficits, and functional deficits exist in individuals who do not meet criteria for mental disorder. Additionally, the co-occurrence of mental disorder (or cognitive disability) and psycholegal deficits is insufficient to establish the bases for a determination of incompetence. A causal connection between the mental disorder or cognitive disability and any noted functional deficits must also be established.

Some jurisdictions may require specific, formal diagnoses to serve as the prerequisite for a determination of incompetence and may limit the types of diagnoses that would be acceptable for such a finding. We take the position here, however, that the symptoms observed in the defendant, rather than the diagnosis *per se,* are of primary importance and need to be highlighted. Evaluators should be careful to consult the relevant competency statutes and guidelines and to offer formal diagnoses when required or when custom dictates, but the focus should remain on the specific symptoms that the defendant manifests. The symptomatic behaviors observed in the defendant will form the basis for the evaluator's inferences regarding whether and the extent to which these symptoms will affect the defendant's context-relevant abilities (e.g., the ability to testify, the ability to relate the facts of the case to the defense attorney, the ability to engage in a plea bargain) and thus her competence to proceed.

BEST PRACTICE
Focus on the defendant's specific symptoms and whether these affect the competence-related abilities required by the defendant's case.

Response Style/ Malingering

The issue of a defendant's response style, especially a malingering response style, must be considered in any forensic evaluation. The

6
chapter

BEST PRACTICE
Weigh information according to the reliability of the source.

evaluator should take care to observe the evaluee's behavior and to compare this to his self-reported behavior in an attempt to determine the degree of consistency or inconsistency. As noted in Chapter 5, forensically relevant instruments developed to assess response style exist, and these should be used when concern arises regarding response style.

The defendant's response style should be taken into consideration in determining how much weight to place on information obtained from the defendant. The evaluator must consider all information, as well as the source of the information, in determining the relevance and importance of each particular piece of data. In general, self-reported information from individuals who show other than honest or straightforward response styles should receive less weight than information from other, more reliable data sources. Although collateral information sources are important in forensic assessments of all types, they become even more important when concerns arise regarding the defendant's response style.

Psycholegal Deficits

As discussed in detail in Chapter 2, a number of psycholegal abilities must be assessed as part of any competency evaluation. Each of these abilities must be evaluated within the context of the specific defendant's case. Any noted deficits in one or more of these competence-related abilities should then be described in terms of how it would affect the defendant's functioning at trial (or during the course of his proceedings).

Understanding

The defendant must demonstrate the ability to factually understand general, legally relevant information. Inability of the defendant to comprehend general information about the arrest process and courtroom proceedings (including the roles of key participants within the legal process), the current charges being faced, the elements of an offense, the general consequences of conviction, or the rights waived in making a guilty plea is usually interpreted as a deficit in factual understanding.

Appreciation

The defendant must demonstrate the ability to apply general, legally relevant information to his own specific case in a rational manner. Inability of the defendant to comprehend or to accurately perceive how specific information regarding the arrest or courtroom process will impact him or his case is usually interpreted as a deficit in appreciation (rational understanding). Deficits in the ability to appreciate may manifest as irrational thinking regarding the likelihood of being found guilty, the consequences of being convicted, the appraisal of available legal defenses and their likely outcomes, the appraisal of whether or not to testify, or the inability to make rational decisions regarding the case.

Reasoning

The defendant must be able to consider and weigh relevant information in a rational, reality-based manner (undistorted by pathology). Inability of the defendant to distinguish more relevant from less relevant information, to weigh and evaluate various legal options and their consequences, to make appropriate comparisons, or to provide reality-based justification for making a particular case-specific decision is usually interpreted as a deficit in the ability to reason.

Assisting Counsel

The defendant must be able to consult with and assist counsel. This generally means that she must have the ability to reason (as just discussed) and to communicate coherently. Inability to consult with counsel, to relate to counsel, to assist in planning legal strategy, to engage in her defense, to challenge witnesses, to testify relevantly, or to manage courtroom behavior may be interpreted as a deficit in the ability to assist counsel.

Decision Making

Decision-making ability is incorporated within other competence-related abilities, such as the ability to appreciate, reason, and assist counsel (as just discussed). Inability of the defendant to make rational decisions regarding specific, relevant aspects of her case is interpreted as a deficit in decision-making ability. Deficits in decision-making ability should be described in terms of their impact on the defendant's ability to appreciate, reason, or assist counsel and/or her functional abilities.

Linkage Between Mental Illness and Context-Relevant Functional Deficits

Once the evaluator has determined that (a) the defendant displays symptoms of mental disorder or cognitive impairment, and (b) that the defendant displays some level of functional deficit in one or more competence-related abilities, the next step involves determining whether the cause of the defendant's competence-related deficits can be attributed to mental disorder or cognitive impairment. It is not enough for mental disorder and functional deficits to co-exist; rather, the mental disorder must be causally related to the defendant's functional deficits. There may be many causes for a defendant's functional deficits; mental illness is only one possible cause of impairment. Situational characteristics (such as lack of sleep or proper nutrition), personal characteristics (such as a lack of experience or education), or response styles are possible alternative explanations that may account for an individual's observed functional deficits. Thus, the evaluator must determine the causal attribution for each relevant deficit since this often dictates the type of remediation necessary.

As legally relevant functional deficits are noted during the assessment, the evaluator should develop hypotheses regarding the cause of the deficits and then collect additional data to test these hypotheses. The evaluator should attempt to confirm or disconfirm the hypotheses regarding the defendant's relevant capacities and behaviors. The goal for the evaluator is to connect the source of information and the raw data that it provides with conclusions regarding relevant psycholegal capacities. Grisso (2003) noted the

BEST
PRACTICE
Determine whether the deficits can be attributed to a mental disorder or cognitive disability or some other cause.

importance of indicating the linkage between mental illness and psycholegal deficits, stating, "examiners must present the logic that links these observations to the specific abilities and capacities with which the law is concerned" (p. 13).

The causal attribution for any noted deficits and the logic and inferences of the evaluator in arriving at the causal attribution should be described for the court. The evaluator can think of the chain of linkages that must be made in the following way (see Figure 6.1):

1. determine whether the defendant displays symptoms of mental illness or cognitive impairment;

2. determine whether the defendant displays competence-related functional deficits;

3. determine whether the cause for the relevant functional deficits can be attributed to mental disorder or cognitive impairment; and

4. for those deficits that can be causally attributed to mental disorder or cognitive impairment, describe the degree of congruence or incongruence between the defendant's functional abilities and deficits and the contextual demands of the case.

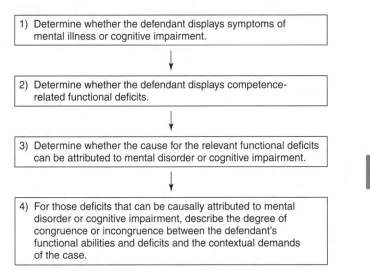

Figure 6.1   Chain of Linkages

Prescriptive Remediation

Many jurisdictions require that forensic mental health evaluators include specific information regarding the prognosis for those defendants opined incompetent. It is important that evaluators be aware of the jurisdictional requirements with respect to the competency evaluation report and that they provide the required information to assist the legal decision maker. Even if not required in a particular jurisdiction, it would still be appropriate to provide this type of information in a court-ordered evaluation.

Evaluators need to consider all relevant factors in making a determination regarding the probability of restoration for a particular defendant. In particular, the defendant's specific functional deficits, treatment history, and previous response to treatment must be considered when offering an opinion on the probability of restoration to competence.

Strategies and Interventions

In addition to general information regarding prognosis and appropriate treatments to restore competency, it is useful for the evaluator to include information about strategies or interventions that may serve to decrease the level of incongruence between a defendant's abilities and the specific demands of the case. That is, evaluators should provide relevant information regarding how

BEST PRACTICE

Appropriate information regarding prescriptive remediation for the competency evaluation report may include

- information regarding the cause of any noted deficits,
- possible interventions or treatment strategies to remediate the deficits,
- facilities where appropriate treatment might be provided,
- an opinion regarding the likelihood of restorability, and
- an estimate of the length of time it might take to restore the defendant to competence.

best to manage a defendant's functional deficits or impairments for the particular legal proceedings.

A defendant's competency is dependent upon his specific abilities and deficits within the context of his case; thus, remedi-

ation can occur either by changing the defendant or by changing the situation in some way. Defendants who have deficits in competence-related abilities that are due to mental illness can be treated for their condition; deficits that can be attributed to being uninformed or misinformed can be remedied by educating the defendant. If a defendant's deficits can be attributed (or partially attributed) to the situation, these might be remedied by changing some relevant aspect of the situation. For example, a defendant with hearing impairment may benefit from the use of an interpreter, a defendant with paranoid psychopathology that interferes with her ability to work with a particular attorney may benefit from a change in counsel, or a defendant with intellectual deficits may benefit from having the proceedings conducted at a slower pace and with simpler language. A change in the situation can serve to decrease the incongruence between a defendant's functional deficits and the abilities required of her to proceed.

The Bases for One's Opinion

Once the evaluator has collected and considered all relevant information, evaluated whether the defendant displays symptoms of mental disorder or cognitive impairment, evaluated whether the defendant displays any competence-related deficits, and determined whether the cause of any noted competence-related deficits can be attributed to the mental disorder or cognitive impairment, the evaluator must then arrive at a conclusion or opinion regarding the defendant's competence to proceed. Even if the evaluator is not required to arrive at an ultimate opinion regarding the defendant's competence, the ways in which the defendant's competence-related abilities are congruent or incongruent with the abilities required to proceed must still be delineated. In addition, information regarding how the defendant's deficits may affect his functional abilities at trial is necessary. Perhaps the most important part of any competency evaluation report is the substantiation of any opinions or conclusions.

Relying on Multiple Sources of Converging Information

Grisso (2003) noted, "no interpretations should be based on any single measure or index alone, no matter what level of reliability or validity may have been demonstrated for it" (p. 48). Thus, the evaluator should rely on multiple sources of converging information in substantiating opinions or conclusions regarding the defendant's competency. The data as a whole should be considered, including self-reported interview data, collateral information sources, testing data, and data obtained from record review. The evaluator should attribute appropriate weight to each piece of information on the basis of the reliability of the data source. Less weight should be attributed to information that is of lower reliability and more weight placed on more reliable information.

In those situations in which the data in a certain domain are inconsistent, the evaluator should consider the reliability of each source of information in making a determination regarding where to place the greater weight. If all sources appear to be equally reliable, but the information provided by each is different, the evaluator should attempt to obtain additional collateral information that would clarify the appropriate information. Of course, this would only be necessary in those instances when that particular piece of information is of primary importance to a competency determination. Conflicting information that is not of primary relevance to a determination of competence can either be noted in the report to court or left out altogether if it is insignificant to the issue of competence.

Outlining the Bases for Opinions

The evaluator should be careful to outline the bases for any opinions or conclusions in the report to court. The data, the source of the data, and the inferences made by the evaluator should be set out so that the legal decision maker is able to follow the logic and reasoning of the evaluator in arriving at conclusions or opinions. This serves to substantiate the opinions of the evaluator as well as educate the legal decision maker. More information about the written report is found in the next chapter.

Report Writing and Testimony | 7

—*The examiner's task is to describe as clearly and accurately as possible that which the defendant knows, understands, believes, or can do.*

(Grisso, 2003, p. 38)

Determination Regarding Whether a Report Is to Be Written

Once the competency assessment has been completed, the evaluator will usually present his opinions and conclusions regarding the issue of CST in a written report. As discussed in Chapter 4, there are some instances when a written report may not be necessary or desired. Thus, it is important that the evaluator consider the referral source and his role, as either a court-ordered or an *ex parte* evaluator, before writing a report.

In a court-ordered evaluation, the forensic evaluator is working for the court (regardless of which party may have initiated the request for evaluation), and a written report is expected. The written report should be sent to the court clerk, as well as the prosecution and defense; thus, all parties are privy to the evaluation report. The court-appointed evaluator will then need to remain available to the court, as he may be subpoenaed to provide testimony about the evaluation and the written report at some later point in time.

In an *ex parte* evaluation, the forensic evaluator is retained by the defense and therefore will communicate his opinions or conclusions regarding the issue of competency to only the retaining attorney. This is initially done in the form of an oral report to the retaining attorney either face-to-face or by phone. This oral report should include the evaluator's opinion regarding the referral question (competence to proceed), as well as relevant information regarding the bases for the opinion. The retaining attorney can then make a decision regarding whether to enter the evaluation results as evidence. The oral report provides the opportunity for the retaining attorney and the evaluator to discuss any issues of legal or psychological significance that might have arisen in the competency evaluation but that would not necessarily be included in a written evaluation report. In addition, it provides the evaluator the opportunity to inform the retaining attorney about any special issues or potential problems that may arise in court as a result of the evaluation findings. Finally, it allows the evaluator the opportunity to suggest appropriate strategies for improving or remediating any noted deficiencies in the interactions between the retaining attorney and the defendant. After this oral report, the retaining attorney will then decide whether the evaluator is to provide a written report.

In those cases in which the opinion of the evaluator does not support a determination of incompetence, a written report may not be requested. It is acceptable practice for attorneys to reject the opinions/conclusions of experts whom they retained and to seek other evaluators' opinions in an attempt to find better support for their cases. Generally, this is when the evaluator's role in the case comes to an end.

In those cases in which a written report is requested, it should be sent to the retaining attorney only (as it is up to the retaining attorney to decide whether to enter the report into evidence or share the results with other parties). In this instance, the evaluator should continue to keep track of all contacts and conversations with the retaining attorney and any other relevant parties, as he may be required to testify about the evaluation and the written report at some later date.

Nature and Purpose of the Written Report

Purpose of the Report

The purpose of the written report is to document relevant information regarding the assessment and procedures, and to communicate the conclusions and opinions formed regarding the referral question. The written report may serve to negate the need for testimony at a competency hearing if all parties accept the findings in the report; thus, reports should be carefully written and informative. In addition, in those cases in which the expert is called to testify at a competency hearing, the written report will usually form the basis for *direct examination* and thus anything in the report may be subject to question on *cross-examination*.

Nature of the Report

Written reports should be thorough yet concise. In discussing the necessary characteristics of forensic reports, Weiner (2006) noted that reports must be clear, relevant, informative, and defensible. In addition, it is important that the written report be appropriate in its scope and focus.

SCOPE AND FOCUS

Relevant ethics codes and guidelines provide guidance regarding the appropriate scope and focus of the written competency evaluation report. Ethical Standard 4.04(a) of the Code of Conduct of the American Psychological Association (2002) states that "psychologists include in written and oral reports and consultations, only information germane to the purpose for which the communication is made" (p. 1066). In addition, section VI. F. 2. of the Specialty Guidelines for Forensic Psychologists (1991) states,

> With respect to evidence of any type, forensic psychologists avoid offering information from their investigations or evaluations that does not bear directly upon the legal purpose of their professional services and that is not critical as support for their product, evidence, or testimony, except where such disclosure is required by law. (Committee on Ethical Guidelines for Forensic Psychologists, 1991, p. 662)

Finally, the American Academy of Psychiatry and the Law (AAPL) Practice Guideline for the Forensic Psychiatric Evaluation of Competence to Stand Trial indicates that "reports should be free of gratuitous comments about defendants' behavior, need for incapacitation, dangerousness, or lack of remorse" and that "reports on

7
chapter

adjudicative competence should not take up other legal matters" (Mossman et al., 2007, p. S51). Thus, competency evaluation reports should focus specifically on the issue of competence to proceed, and information that is not directly relevant to this issue should be limited.

CLARITY

In writing competency evaluation reports, it is necessary to consider the audience for the report and to write accordingly. It is inappropriate to assume that technical jargon used to communicate with other mental health professionals will be understood by legal professionals. Thus, reports should be written in a clear, concise manner using as little technical jargon as possible. In those (relatively few) instances when technical jargon must be used (such as when it is necessary to justify legal or clinical relevance), it is appropriate to include a definition or description of what is meant by the term immediately following its use. Even relatively common terms, such as hallucinations or delusions, are often misunderstood by non–mental health professionals.

Weiner (2006) offers the following advice:

> The written report itself should be as clear and conversational as the psychologist can make it. This means using unstilted and uncomplicated language that will be comfortable for [evaluators] to repeat on the witness stand, that will be comprehensible to judge and jury, and that will limit a cross-examining attorney's opportunities to badger them with questions about what their statements mean. (p. 645)

In addition, Weiner cautions that the evaluator should concentrate on writing about the *person* who was evaluated, rather than about psychological processes, since "impersonal descriptions of psychological processes often go hand in hand with jargon" (p. 645). For example, a statement such as "concentration was intact" does not communicate as clearly as "Mr. Z was able to demonstrate appropriate concentration by staying focused during a lengthy discussion of his charges and contributing detailed information without becoming distracted."

RELEVANCE

Section VII. F. of the Specialty Guidelines for Forensic Psychologists (1991) states, "forensic psychologists are aware that their essential role as expert to the court is to assist the trier of fact to understand the evidence or to determine a fact in issue" (Committee on Ethical Guidelines for Forensic Psychologists, 1991, p. 665). The second draft of these Specialty Guidelines, which are still under revision at the time of writing, elaborate that evaluators are to provide information most relevant to the psycholegal issue: In reports and testimony, forensic practitioners typically provide information about examinees' functional abilities, capacities, knowledge, and beliefs, depending on the psycholegal issue in question, and address their opinions and recommendations to the factors identified in the court order, law, rule, or contract relevant to the matter. In addition, the AAPL Practice Guideline for the Forensic Psychiatric Evaluation of Competence to Stand Trial states that "the report must provide a meaningful response to the competence inquiry" and "should convey all relevant information concisely, allowing the reader to apprehend the facts and reasoning the expert used in formulating the opinion" (Mossman et al., 2007, p. S48). Thus, the written forensic report should address all factors relevant to the issue of competency. As discussed in Chapter 4, evaluators should be knowledgeable about relevant legal standards, statutes, and jurisdictional case law regarding competence. Their written reports should address these relevant standards and jurisdictional competency requirements and summarize those features of the defendant that bear directly on the issue of competency.

●
◎ **BEST**
 PRACTICE
Address the relevant legal standards and jurisdictional competency requirements in the written report.

During the course of a competency evaluation it is common to accumulate much more information than is needed to address the issue of

7
chapter

competence. As a general rule, only information that bears directly on the issue of competence should be included in the written report. Grisso (1988) advocates a "problem-focused" approach to deciding what information to include in a written report:

> The examiner can determine the extent to which information from hospital records, criminal records, and a social history must be described in a given case by applying a simple 'problem-focused' question: *'Does the piece of information I am preparing to report act as an important basis for the reasoning I will use in arriving at one of the competency evaluation's objectives?'* If the answer is no, the piece of information usually should not be included. (p. 74, italics in original)

INFORMATIVE

The written report should be informative and educational. Data and inferences should be presented and explained in a way that is easy to understand by those who are not forensic mental health professionals. The report can be used as a forum to educate the reader about relevant psychological concepts and their relation to the issue of competency. Brief descriptions of psychological tests or forensic assessment instruments (FAIs) and the abilities that they measure can be provided to assist the reader in understanding the relevance of test results to the issue of competency.

To guard against information overkill (and an unnecessarily lengthy report), it is important to carefully consider which pieces of information to include. Those pieces of information that are directly relevant to the issue of competence or the inferences made should be included, and inferences should be explained. In addition, it is important to indicate the source from which the information was obtained. Informative and educational reports are those that lead the reader through the relevant pieces of information that were considered and weighed by the evaluator. Furthermore, the report should delineate the expert's thought processes in coming to an opinion or conclusion regarding the defendant's competency.

BEST PRACTICE
Educate the reader by including relevant information and clearly explaining how it was used to reach an opinion or conclusion regarding the defendant's competency.

To avoid the possibility of having the results of an evaluation conducted within one context misapplied to another context, Skeem, Golding, and Emke-Francis (2003) suggest the inclusion of a summary statement such as,

> **BEWARE**
> Opinions and conclusions may be challenged in court on the basis of the written report.

> At the time of this report, the defendant has a good relationship with his attorney and his capacity to engage in rational choice of trial strategies, with the assistance of counsel, was unaffected by his mental disorder. Should the context of his case change, I would need to evaluate this defendant in order to render a reliable and current opinion as to his competency. (p. 187)

DEFENSIBLE

Written reports are discoverable and may be entered into evidence; thus, evaluators may be held accountable for every statement made in their reports. For this reason, it is imperative that evaluators choose their words carefully and thoughtfully and be able to defend the opinions and conclusions set out in their reports. Weiner (2006) cautioned that "forensic psychologists should limit their written reports to statements they will feel comfortable hearing read aloud in the courtroom and to conclusions they feel able to defend against reasonable challenge" (p. 639).

Written reports should present information in as defensible a manner as possible. Weiner (2006, pp. 648–650) delineated four ways in which to guard against potential pitfalls in giving expert witness testimony on the basis of written reports:

1. Evaluators should use description, rather than categorization, when offering conclusions about their evaluees. Thus, it is more defensible to say, "This defendant shows many features in common with people who have developed a stress disorder subsequent to a traumatic experience" than "this defendant has a posttraumatic stress disorder."

2. Relative statements about evaluees should be favored over absolute statements. Thus, statements that a

defendant is more likely or less likely than other people to show certain characteristics are more defensible than absolute, black-and-white statements.

3. Evaluators should avoid writing statements that rule out certain conditions or events. The fact that an evaluator's data do not provide evidence for a particular condition does not eliminate the possibility of its existence. Therefore, evaluators should be careful not to overstate their findings and should place the emphasis on what their findings demonstrate as probably being present rather than on what can be ruled out. In those situations, however, when reporting of negative findings is warranted, evaluators should exercise caution in drawing conclusions from these findings.

4. Evaluators should avoid including illustrative test responses in their reports. This last point pertains to the selection of responses from critical items of self-report inventories or other psychological tests wherein the meanings of individual items are of little significance by themselves but, rather, must be interpreted when combined into multi-item scales. Selecting responses from critical items belonging to tests of this format for inclusion in the report leaves the evaluator open to questions about the meaning of individual test responses. This, however, is different from including illustrative responses from FAIs developed specifically for use in the evaluation of competency. In this situation, illustrative responses may be helpful in delineating the defendant's thought processes and competence-related abilities.

Contents of the Written Report

We recognize that there are many ways to organize a report; however, any competency evaluation report should include the types of information that are encompassed by the organizational structure presented in this section.

Relevant Case and Referral Information

The report should begin by providing relevant case and defendant information. Typically included at the beginning of the report are the defendant's name, defendant's date of birth, case number, date(s) of the evaluation, and the date that the report was written. In addition, relevant referral information should be provided, including

- the referral source,
- the referral question(s) (i.e., CST),
- the defendant's charge(s), and
- the reason for the referral (information obtained from the referral source regarding the types of statements or behaviors the defendant displayed that raised the issue of competency).

BEST PRACTICE

Include the following in competency evaluation reports:

- relevant case and referral information,
- notification information,
- summary of alleged offense(s),
- data sources,
- background information,
- clinical assessment,
- forensic assessment, and
- summary and recommendations.

Notification

This section of the report should contain a brief summary of the notification or informed consent of the defendant (see Chapter 5 and Appendix C). In addition, statements regarding the extent to which the defendant appeared to understand the notification information, whether the defendant agreed or refused to participate in the evaluation, and whether the defendant signed a *notification of rights* form should be included in this section.

Summary of Alleged Offense(s)

This section should include a summary of the alleged offense(s) as described in the police report or other official documentation. As will be discussed in a later section on inappropriate report contents, the defendant's version of the alleged offense(s) should not be included in the report. This section should be reserved for a description of the charges and allegations as depicted by official sources of documentation or as

7
chapter

provided by the referral source. In addition, the source of the information should be noted.

Data Sources

This section should contain a list of all data sources consulted for the purposes of the assessment. This would include

- medical, criminal, educational, or other records that were reviewed (record dates and sources of information should be clearly identified);
- collateral contacts who were interviewed (including the date, name of the contact, amount of time spent interviewing, and whether the interview was conducted in person or by phone);
- observations of interactions between the defendant and defense counsel (including dates and length of time observed);
- and the date(s) and length of time for which the defendant was interviewed.

In addition, the presence of any individuals (such as defense counsel or correctional officers) during any of the interviews can be noted.

To assist the reader in surveying all data sources at a glance, it is also useful to include a list of any psychological tests, forensically relevant instruments, or competency assessment instruments administered for the purposes of the evaluation in this section. Dates and administration times can also be included.

Finally, it is also useful to include a list of those data sources that were requested but that were not forthcoming and so were not considered by the evaluator in arriving at an opinion regarding the defendant's competence.

Background Information

This section should include relevant information about the defendant's background. As discussed earlier in this chapter, it is important to carefully consider the amount of information (as well as the amount of detail) provided in this section of the report. Using

Grisso's problem-focused approach—including only information relevant to the reasoning regarding an opinion on the defendant's competency or competence-related abilities—appears to be a useful strategy. In addition, it is important to accurately attribute information included in this section of the report to its appropriate source (e.g., defendant's self-report, medical records, collateral interview).

Clinical Assessment

This section of the report should include information about the defendant's clinical presentation, mental status, and psychological functioning. Observations of the defendant's behavior should be included in this section, especially if they bear directly on the evaluator's inferences regarding the defendant's competence-related abilities or deficits. Descriptions of and conclusions about the defendant's psychological functioning and the presence of any mental illness or psychiatric symptoms should also be included.

If psychological tests were administered as part of the competency evaluation, descriptions of these tests and the performance of the defendant on these instruments should be included in this section of the report. The evaluator should be clear about the link between the ability or characteristic measured by the test and the defendant's psychological functioning. In the next section of the report, forensic assessment, any psychological testing results will need to be directly tied to inferences regarding the defendant's competence-related abilities or deficits.

Forensic Assessment

This section is the most important and comprises the "meat" of the report. A description of the defendant's competence-related abilities and deficits should be provided. In addition, the question of malingering or response style should be addressed, even if only to indicate that there appeared to be no evidence of malingering on the part of the defendant. Of course, if malingering was indicated, more detail about response style and any formal evaluation of malingering should be described. If a competency assessment instrument was used to structure the evaluation or to supplement competence-related

⊙ **BEST**
PRACTICE

Give priority to the forensic assessment section, which should include

- a description of competence-related abilities and deficits,
- cause of any noted deficits,
- the impact of symptoms on the defendant's performance or participation in the case,
- possible prescriptive remediation,
- conclusions or opinions regarding each of the jurisdictional criteria, and
- prognosis for restorability.

inquiries, this section should provide a brief description of the instrument(s) used, as well as a description of the defendant's performance in terms of her competence-related abilities and deficits.

DESCRIPTION OF COMPETENCE-RELATED ABILITIES AND DEFICITS

To structure the presentation of information regarding the defendant's competence-related abilities and deficits, it is often helpful to include the jurisdictional definition, standard, or criteria for competency. This way, the evaluator can provide a description of the defendant's relevant abilities and deficits for each component of the legal standard. For example, in providing information about the defendant's understanding of the nature or object of the proceedings (the first prong of the Federal standard for competency), the evaluator could describe the defendant's abilities and deficits regarding understanding of the arrest process, the nature and severity of the current charges, the role of key participants, the legal process, pleas, court procedure, and any other relevant inquiry.

CAUSE OF DEFICITS

Once a description of the defendant's competence-related abilities and deficits has been provided, the evaluator then must explain the cause of any noted deficits (e.g., mental illness, malingering, situational factors, other). The bases for the evaluator's conclusions or opinions on this matter should be clearly delineated. Providing examples of the defendant's inadequate or impaired competence-related abilities (e.g., understanding, appreciation, reasoning, assisting counsel, decision making) may assist the evaluator in describing these deficits. In the case of mental disorder, it is not sufficient to merely establish that it co-exists with psycholegal deficits; a causal connection between the two must be established and should be clearly described in the report.

IMPACT OF SYMPTOMS ON PERFORMANCE/PARTICIPATION

For those deficits that are caused by mental illness, the evaluator should then describe how the relevant symptoms would affect the defendant's performance or participation in the case. This is where knowledge regarding the expectations and capacities required of the defendant for the specific legal proceeding becomes important. When the evaluator is unsure about the specific expectations or abilities required of the defendant, it is appropriate to use conditional statements that set out how the defendant's functional abilities at trial may be affected by his deficits. For example, a defendant whose depression causes an inability to concentrate for more than brief periods of time may have difficulty following lengthy trial proceedings but may remain focused during a short trial. Thus, if the evaluator is uninformed about how long the defendant's trial is expected to last, a conditional statement may be included in the report regarding the defendant's concentration abilities in relation to the length of the proceedings.

PRESCRIPTIVE REMEDIATION

If prescriptive remediation for any noted deficits can be offered, a description of this should be included in this section of the report. For example, if the evaluator determines that a defendant with low IQ is unable to understand lengthy, complicated sentences but is able to comprehend short sentences, then including a recommendation to use concise language with an uncomplicated structure and to define uncommon or difficult words for the defendant would be appropriate.

CONCLUSIONS OR OPINIONS
This section of the report should also contain the evaluator's conclusions or opinions regarding each of the jurisdictional criteria for competency. If comfortable for the evaluator or required by the jurisdiction, the ultimate issue of competency (to be discussed later) may be addressed. Of course, the bases for all opinions rendered should be included.

RESTORABILITY
Finally, many jurisdictions require the evaluator to include information in the report about the defendant's prognosis for restorability, the type of treatments required and available for restoration, appropriate treatment facilities, and an estimate of the amount of time needed to restore a defendant to competency for those defendants opined incompetent to proceed. Thus, this and other relevant jurisdictionally required information should be included in this section of the report.

Summary and Recommendations
This final section of the report will offer a brief summary of the evaluator's conclusions and opinions. Brevity is expected in this section, as detailed descriptions of the information provided here should have been included in earlier sections of the report. A brief description of the defendant's competence-related abilities and deficits should be provided along with the cause of the deficits and their relationship to the defendant's functional abilities at trial (e.g., how they will impact the defendant's participation in her proceedings). A formal diagnosis would be included in this section of the report if one is required or expected. In addition, the evaluator may offer an *ultimate legal opinion* regarding the defendant's competency, if acceptable or expected, in this section of the report. Finally, a brief summary of prescriptive remediation or remediation potential should be offered for those defendants with significant competence-related deficits.

Linkages Between Mental Illness, Competence-Related Deficits, and the Defendant's Functional Abilities at Trial or Within the Context of the Legal Proceedings

The issue of the linkages between mental illness, competence-related deficits, and functional abilities at trial (or for the purposes of the defendant's proceedings) has been mentioned earlier in this chapter but its importance will be highlighted again here.

In a survey of forensic diplomates of the American Board of Forensic Psychology (ABPP), Borum and Grisso (1996) found that 90% of respondents agreed that detailing the link between mental illness and competence-related deficits in competency reports was either recommended or essential. However, an examination of CST reports from two states indicated that only 27% of the reports provided an explanation regarding how the defendant's mental illness influenced his competence-related abilities (Robbins, Waters, & Herbert, 1997). Further, in another study, only 10% of competency evaluation reports reviewed provided an explanation regarding how the defendant's psychopathology compromised required competence-related abilities (Skeem et al., 1998). In addition to the issue of the linkage between mental illness and competence-related deficits, the extant research also indicates that examiners rarely (Skeem et al., 1998) or never (Robbins et al., 1997) assess the congruence between a defendant's abilities and the specific case context.

This discrepancy between what experts deem recommended or essential for competency evaluation reports and what is actually routinely contained in these reports is concerning, especially in light of the significant weight that these reports are given by judges in making competency determinations. It has been widely reported that judicial decisions regarding competency rarely deviate from the evaluator's opinion or conclusion. Empirical research examining rates of agreement between judicial decisions of competency and examiner opinions show that upward of 90% of the time—indeed, agreement rates as high as 99.6% have been reported—judges are in agreement with the evaluator's opinion regarding competency (Hart & Hare, 1992; Reich & Tookey, 1986; Zapf, Hubbard, Cooper, Wheeles, & Ronan, 2004).

Thus, the highest standards of practice must be adhered to by forensic evaluators if their reports will have such a strong influence on the disposition of the competency issue (see Zapf et al., 2004). Given that the nature and reliability of the evaluator's reasoning become critical components of the adjudication process, they must be spelled out accordingly. As Heilbrun, Marczyk, and DeMatteo (2002) suggest, the evaluator can use contingency statements in the form of "if x, then y; if not x, then z" to assist the audience in understanding the links between clinical observations, the evaluator's reasoning, and the conclusions that he or she reaches" (p. 53). Such careful delineation between mental illness and competence-related deficits and between competence-related deficits and functional abilities within the specific context of the defendant's case will serve to elevate the quality and utility of the report.

Skeem and her colleagues (1998) devised a coding scheme for evaluating the extent to which the relationship between symptomatology and competence-related abilities was described by evaluators in their reports. We replicate her coding scheme here, as we believe that it clearly demonstrates the types of statements that evaluators need to make to substantiate their opinions (Skeem & Golding, 1998, p. 363):

- Cases in which the evaluator simply described the competency domain as being impaired but did not provide any information regarding the relationship of this impairment to the defendant's symptoms were characterized by statements such as, "the accused is unable to relate to her attorney."

- Cases where the evaluator presented quotes from the defendant or examples that merely *implied* a link between impairment and psychopathology were characterized by statements such as, "the defendant stated that the role of her attorney is 'a lot of persons on your property, the private-side for my defense some friends and family' [sic]."

- Cases in which the evaluator *asserted* a relationship by attributing impairment to psychopathology without specifically describing the relationship were characterized by statements such as, "the defendant's ability to relate to her attorney will be compromised by her delusional thought processes."

- Cases where the author *substantiated* the relationship by specifying how the impairment was caused by psychopathology were characterized by statements such as, "the defendant is committed to a delusional system that includes a belief that her attorney is receiving commands from God to ensure that she is punished. This delusion compromises her trust in and ability to relate to her attorney."

Inappropriate Report Contents

The Defendant's Version of the Circumstances Surrounding the Offense

The issue of inquiring about the defendant's version of the circumstances surrounding the time of the offense was addressed in Chapter 5. There, we concluded that a functional evaluation of competency requires that the evaluator inquire about the charges and allegations; however, we also noted that caution must be exercised by evaluators in writing the evaluation report so as not to include potentially incriminating information provided by the defendant. General statements regarding whether the defendant's account of events differs substantially from official accounts, and whether this reflects an incapacity or deficit on the part of the defendant, should be used instead of a summary of the defendant' s account or the defendant's verbatim answers. The careful consideration on the part of evaluators about what to include and what to

BEWARE
Be careful not to include potentially incriminating information provided by the defendant in the report.

leave out of the report can act as an added protection against any potential prosecutorial misuse of the information obtained during a competency evaluation.

Other Legal Issues

In many jurisdictions, competency evaluations and assessments of mental state at the time of the offense are often ordered simultaneously. In this situation, the evaluator may choose to prepare a separate report for each referral question or to address both referral questions within the same report, as determined by personal preference or by jurisdictional requirement. If the evaluator chooses or is required to address both legal issues within the same report, the aforementioned warnings with respect to including the defendant's version of the events surrounding the time of the offenses(s) in the report still apply. If separate reports are issued, the evaluator should ensure that no information or opinions regarding mental state at the time of the offense is included in the competency assessment report.

The evaluator should be careful to address only those referral questions that have been asked and to refrain from offering unsolicited information about other, possibly relevant, legal issues in the competency evaluation report. Opinions or conclusions regarding a defendant's future risk for violent behavior, or any other legal or psychological issue, have no place in a competency evaluation report.

The "Ultimate Issue" Issue

The question of whether to speak to the ultimate legal issue (i.e., whether the defendant is competent or incompetent) has been a long-standing subject of much debate within the field (see, for example, Grisso, 1986, 2003; Melton, Petrila, Poythress, & Slobogin, 1987, 1997, 2007; Morse, 1978; Slobogin, 1989). Those who believe that forensic evaluators should not offer an opinion on the ultimate legal issue argue that evaluators can offer scientific and clinical opinions, but that legal decisions (which encompass moral and social considerations) are beyond their area of expertise. To offer an opinion on the ultimate legal issue of a defendant's competency would be to intrude on the role of the legal fact-finder. Grisso (2003) noted that the question of "*how much of a deficit in abilities is enough to justify the restriction of individual liberties*" requires a social and moral judgment, as it cannot be answered without applying personal values (p. 15, italics in original).

On the other hand, those who believe that forensic evaluators should offer an opinion on the ultimate legal issue argue that the fact-finder should be able to consider all available information, including ultimate opinions of forensic evaluators, and weigh the evidence accordingly in arriving at a final determination on the issue. No requirement exists that the fact-finder accept the evaluator's opinion on the ultimate issue. In addition, stating an opinion on the ultimate issue might assist the fact-finder in following the evaluator's testimony, since the direction of the testimony is made obvious.

Empirical evidence suggests that this issue is far from settled. Approximately 25% of the ABPP forensic diplomates surveyed by Borum and Grisso (1996) indicated that ultimate opinions were to be avoided, whereas the other 75% were either neutral on the issue or believed it was important to offer such opinions. Robbins and colleagues (1997) found that upward of 90% of the competency evaluation reports they examined offered ultimate opinions, and Skeem and her colleagues (1998) found ultimate opinions offered in about 75% of the reports they examined.

In some jurisdictions, ultimate opinions are expected or required, whereas in others they may be prohibited or discouraged. In many jurisdictions, the court-appointed expert is required to check a box on the evaluation form indicating whether the defendant "is" or "is not" competent. In this situation, a court-ordered assessment and the requirements of the law would override ethical considerations against providing an ultimate opinion. In addition, the evaluator who believes that the opinion is too complex to simply check a box should include any necessary stipulations near the box and in the attached report.

Each evaluator must consider the requirements of the relevant jurisdiction, as well as her training, experience, and beliefs in

7
chapter

determining whether to offer an opinion on the ultimate legal issue. Those evaluators who are not comfortable with offering an ultimate opinion could write their reports in such a way as to separate the legal issue (competency) from the psychological issues affecting the legal issue. These psychological issues could then be described in detail, and the relationship between the psychological issues to the legal question delineated in the report. Those evaluators who are comfortable with offering an ultimate opinion should do so (if jurisdictional requirements permit) but must also ensure that their logic, inferences, and thought processes in arriving at a conclusion on the ultimate issue are laid out in the report.

Testimony

What follows is a brief discussion of some issues relevant to the presentation of competency evaluation findings through expert witness testimony. The reader should consult other sources for more detailed information on preparing for and delivering effective expert testimony (e.g., Bank & Packer, 2007; Brodsky, 1991, 1999, 2004; Ewing, 2003; Gutheil, 1998; Hess, 2006; Tsushima & Anderson, 1996; Ziskin & Faust, 1995).

Preparation for Taking the Stand

A forensic evaluator may be subpoenaed (in the case of court-ordered evaluations) or asked (in the case of *ex parte* evaluations) to testify at a competency hearing. At this point, the evaluator will need to adequately prepare to take the stand as an expert. The written report will usually serve as the basis for direct examination and be entered into evidence; thus, any information contained in the written report will also be subject to cross-examination. Given the significant weight attached to the written report, the evaluator should carefully review the report as many times as necessary to become familiar with all the material contained within it. The evaluator should review all other materials that were relied on for the evaluation (i.e., the data sources listed in the written report). In addition, the evaluator should refamiliarize himself with the psychometric properties for any psychological tests, forensically relevant instruments, and FAIs administered as part of the assessment. In cases in which the evaluator was privately retained, he may wish to check with retaining counsel to determine whether any other information sources should be reviewed (e.g., sometimes the retaining attorney will ask the expert to review the opinions and conclusions of the opposing side's expert).

If the evaluator conducted an *ex parte* evaluation, a pretrial conference with the retaining attorney is common. During this meeting, the retaining attorney will generally tell the evaluator the theory of the case, how she would like the evaluator's information presented, and any relevant information regarding what the opposing side may try to prove. In addition, general information about the courtroom process may be discussed. Multiple copies of the evaluator's *curriculum vita* should be provided, as this will be used to structure the retaining attorney's questions regarding the evaluator's qualifications and to have the evaluator qualified as an expert. In addition, the evaluator should inform the retaining attorney about any possible weaknesses in his opinion or conclusions as well as any possible weaknesses in the opposing side's opinion (if known). The attorney may ask practice questions (both direct and cross-examination) to help prepare the evaluator for testimony.

If the evaluator conducted a court-ordered evaluation, a pretrial conference usually does not occur. The evaluator should arrive somewhat early for the hearing and wait outside the courtroom until called to testify. Even if the *curriculum vita* has already been sent to the court ahead of time, the evaluator should bring additional copies to the hearing.

On the Witness Stand

In general, the evaluator should not be present in the courtroom for anything other than his testimony. In some instances, the evaluator will be asked to stay in the courtroom and to listen to the testimony of other witnesses, but he should not do so unless specifically requested.

The sources listed at the beginning of this section provide detailed information on many aspects of courtroom demeanor. Briefly, it is appropriate to dress conservatively in the courtroom and to focus attention on the judge (or the jurors, if applicable). The

7
chapter

INFO

In qualifying the expert, the court considers

● education,

● experience, and

● the evaluation procedure and methods used.

evaluator should use clear, conversational language and should explain unfamiliar concepts, using lay language rather than professional jargon. Deference to the judge and courtesy toward the attorneys should be displayed.

After being sworn in, the evaluator will be asked questions about his credentials for the purposes of being qualified as an expert. Three basic factors will be considered in determining whether an evaluator should be qualified as an expert—education, experience, and the evaluation procedure and methods used—although the judge is the final arbiter of this issue. Often, evaluators will be asked (either on direct or cross-examination) about how many times they have appeared as a witness for the prosecution and for the defense, so it is helpful if the evaluator has anticipated this line of questioning.

When being questioned, the evaluator should speak in a confident manner and loud enough for the judge (or jury) to hear. If a question is unclear, the evaluator should ask that it be repeated or reworded. The evaluator should answer only what has been asked without volunteering additional information. When an objection has been made, the evaluator should stop speaking and wait for the judge to make a ruling. If the evaluator does not have a particular piece of knowledge, the answer should be an honest one: "I do not know."

The purpose of the evaluator's testimony is to educate the fact-finder about the relevant issues and to provide data, inferences, and opinions. Just as in the written report, the data should be set out and the inferences explained, so that the evaluator's logic in arriving at conclusions and opinions is evident.

Cross-Examination

Cross-examination can be a stressful experience; however, the expert should maintain a calm demeanor throughout. Cross-examination allows the evaluator the opportunity to reiterate points made during her direct examination testimony. The sources listed at the beginning of this section deal with cross-examination testimony in great detail and should be consulted by the evaluator before testifying in court.

Briefly, cross-examining attorneys may use multiple tactics in an attempt to attack or discredit the expert witness, her testimony, and the opinion on trial competence. The main objective of the evaluator is to remain calm and focused on the data. If questions are long or confusing, the evaluator should ask that they be repeated. When asked a "hypothetical" question, the evaluator should be clear about what data are provided in the question and should state whether more data are needed to answer the question. If the cross-examining attorney misstates a fact, the evaluator should clarify the facts before answering the question (e.g., being careful not to let the attorney put words in her mouth). If the evaluator misspeaks on the stand, she should indicate that she spoke in error and correct the error. If the cross-examining attorney asks a question for which a yes or no answer is demanded, and the evaluator believes that this type of answer is not appropriate, she should indicate to the court that a yes or no answer would be misleading.

As a general statement, testimony, whether it be on direct or cross, is most effective when the evaluator presents the data and inferences in a clear, concise manner in language that is easy to understand while focusing attention on the trier of fact. It is important that the evaluator maintain a calm demeanor on the witness stand and speak in a confident manner about the evaluation and the data. Effective presentation offers the evaluator the opportunity to share his knowledge and to educate others about issues relevant to the defendant's fitness for trial.

7
chapter

Appendix | A

Attorney CST Questionnaire*

TO (Client's Attorney): _____

FROM (Evaluator): _____ DATE: _____

Your client, _____, (Docket # _____) has been referred to me for evaluation of competence to stand trial. I would greatly appreciate your completion of the following form, which will provide valuable assistance in conducting this evaluation. Please do not hesitate to phone me if you have any questions. My contact information is as follows:

Telephone _____ FAX _____ E-mail _____

Agency & Address _____

Who brought your client's competency to the attention of the court?

☐ Myself   ☐ Prosecuting   ☐ Court's own   ☐ Probation
                   attorney   motion   officer

☐ Detention staff ☐ Arresting   ☐ Client's   ☐ Other: _____
                      officers   family

---

*This form represents a slight modification of an adaptation by Grisso (2005) to the original form developed by Kruh, Sullivan, & Dunham (2001). Permission from both Tom Grisso and Ivan Kruh was obtained to include this form as an appendix.

Original version: Kruh, I., Sullivan, L., & Dunham, J. (2001). *Respondent's attorney competency questionnaire*. State of Washington Department of Social and Health Services, Child Study and Treatment Center.

Adapted version: Grisso, T. (2005). Attorney CST questionnaire. In *Evaluating juveniles' adjudicative competence: A guide for clinical practice*. Sarasota, FL: Professional Resource Press.

What factors, if any, contributed to the perceived need for a competency evaluation?

Check all that apply   *Describe factors checked*

☐ History of mental illness   _____

☐ History of psychiatric medication   _____

☐ History of psychiatric hospitalization   _____

☐ History of counseling/therapy   _____

☐ History of mental retardation   _____

☐ Difficulty communicating with client   _____

☐ Client's unusual behavior   _____

☐ Other   _____

One aspect of competency is the client's understanding of the charges and the associated possible dispositions. To assist me in evaluating this, please describe:

The charges against your client: _____

The nature of the dispositions that your client might face, given these charges and your client's past record: _____

_____

_____

_____

Please describe any collateral consequences or added stressors in the client's life that I should consider when interacting with this client:

_____

_____

_____

_____

_____

_____

Another aspect of competency is the client's ability to assist counsel and to manage the attorney–client relationship in a way that does not detract from the opportunity to develop the defense. Below, please indicate any factors that you have seen detract from these objectives and describe how.

Check all that apply   *Describe factors checked*

☐ Easily confused   _____

☐ Detached or indifferent   _____

☐ Depressed   _____

☐ Hostile, aggressive, defiant   _____

☐ Inattentive or distracted   _____

☐ Immature or childlike   _____

☐ Difficulty communicating things   _____

☐ Difficulty understanding you   _____

☐ Difficulty retaining information   _____

☐ Disorganized speech   _____

☐ Peculiar/Odd statements or beliefs   _____

☐ Seeing/Hearing things not present   _____

☐ Very bizarre behavior   _____

☐ Other   _____

☐ Have observed nothing detracting from attorney–client interaction

Competency is in part a comparison of the client's abilities to the demands of his or her case. Please describe the likelihood of the following demands for this client's case (circle one response for each).

1. Is likely to have   No   Unlikely   Don't know   Likely   Definitely
   to make a
   decision about a
   plea agreement

2. Evidence against   No   Unlikely   Don't know   Likely   Definitely
   client is unclear
   and the defense
   largely depends
   on the client's
   ability to provide
   information

3. Case will involve   No   Unlikely   Don't know   Likely   Definitely
   many adverse
   witnesses

4. Client will need   No   Unlikely   Don't know   Likely   Definitely
   to testify in the
   case

5. The pre-   No   Unlikely   Don't know   Likely   Definitely
   adjudication
   process will be
   lengthy

6. The adjudication   No   Unlikely   Don't know   Likely   Definitely
   hearing will be
   lengthy

7. The adjudication   No   Unlikely   Don't know   Likely   Definitely
   hearing will be
   complex (e.g.,
   difficult to follow,
   complicated
   evidence)

Appendix | B

Collateral and Third-Party Information Sources

Records and Written Documents	Interview Sources
Previous competency evaluations	Defense attorney
Witness statements	Spouses or partners
Transcripts from depositions or hearings	Roommates
Police reports	Neighbors
Crime reports	Family members
Crime scene evidence	Employers, supervisors, and colleagues
Autopsy reports	Police/arresting officers
Mental health records	Parole or probation officers
Medical records	Jail staff (medical, mental health, correctional, or treatment staff)
Criminal records	Community case managers

(Continued)

Records and Written Documents	Interview Sources
Juvenile criminal records	Hospital or correctional facility staff
School records	Medical professionals who have evaluated/treated defendant
Employment records	Mental health professionals who have evaluated/treated defendant
Military records	Others who have had recent contact with the defendant
Diaries, journals, or letters	
Jail or prison records	

Appendix C

Sample Notification Form

Nature & Purpose: I have been asked to evaluate you with regard to your competence to stand trial. The purpose of this evaluation is to provide the court with information regarding your abilities to participate in your trial. This evaluation may involve any or all of the following: (a) talking with you about your history, (b) talking with other people who know you about your history, (c) reading reports and other file information about you, (d) talking with your attorney, and (e) having you complete psychological tests.

Extent: In addition to some general questions about your history, I will be asking you some questions about your relationship with your attorney; your understanding of the legal system, such as what goes on at trial; and questions about the charges against you.

Amount of time: The entire evaluation will most likely take me about 2 weeks to conduct and I may need to speak with you again after we speak today.

Psychological report: I will be writing a psychological report, which will be sent to the court and will also be made available to your attorney and the prosecutor. If the judge orders a hearing on the issue of your competency, I might be called to testify in court.

How information will be used: Because this is an evaluation of your competence to stand trial, nothing you tell me now about your case or what you did can be used against you at your trial. The information that we discuss for this evaluation can only be used at the hearing on the issue of your competency, if there is one. Otherwise, this information cannot be used against you when you go to trial.

Confidentiality: I am a psychologist, but our relationship will not be like the typical relationship between a psychologist and client. Usually, psychologists are required to keep everything that is said confidential. That is not the case in our relationship. I will be conducting an evaluation and everything that you tell me can be put into my report. I cannot keep anything that you tell me confidential between only you and I.

Duty to warn or protect: If you were to tell me that you had plans to hurt yourself or someone else, I will need to tell your lawyer, and possibly others, about this. Also, if you tell me that you are currently involved in abusing a minor (or an elderly person), I am required by law to inform child protective services (or elder protective services) about this.

Right to refuse: The court ordered this evaluation and, therefore, you do not have the right to refuse to participate. Should you decline to answer my questions, I may still need to provide a written report to the court.

or, for *ex parte* evaluations,

Your attorney has asked me to conduct this evaluation. Should you decline to participate, you will need to speak with your attorney about the benefits and risks of doing so.

The purpose of this evaluation, as summarized above, has been explained to me and I understand the limited confidentiality that applies. I agree to participate in the evaluation at this time.

Signature of Defendant: _____

Date: _____

Witness to verbal consent: _____

Date: _____

Appendix | D

List of Relevant Competence-Related Domains and Areas of Inquiry

Domain	Subdomain
Capacity to understand the arrest process	Ability to provide an account of police behavior at the time of arrest Comprehension of the *Miranda* warning Confession behavior (influence of mental disorder, suggestibility, and so forth on confession)
Capacity to comprehend and appreciate the charges or allegations	Factual knowledge of the charges (ability to report charge label) Understanding of the behaviors to which the charges refer Comprehension of the police version of events Understanding of the severity of the charges
Capacity to disclose to counsel pertinent facts, events, and states of mind	Ability to provide a reasonable account of one's behavior around the time of the alleged offense Ability to provide information about one's state of mind around the time of the alleged offense Ability to provide an account of the behavior of relevant others around the time of the alleged offense
Capacity to comprehend and appreciate the range and nature of potential penalties that may be imposed in the proceedings	Knowledge of penalties that could be imposed (e.g., knowledge of the relevant sentence label associated with the charge, such as "5 to life") Comprehension of the seriousness of the charges and potential sentences

(Continued)

Domain	Subdomain
Capacity to appreciate the likely outcome of the proceedings	Capacity to provide a realistic appraisal of the likelihood of being convicted Understanding of the finality of the court's decision and the authority of the court
Basis knowledge of legal strategies and options	Understanding of the meaning of alternative pleas (e.g., guilty, not guilty, NGRI, GBMI, nolo contendere, as applicable) Knowledge of the plea bargaining process
Capacity to engage in reasoned choice of legal strategies and options (decision making)	Capacity to comprehend legal advice Capacity to participate in planning a defense strategy Ability to deal appropriately with disagreements with counsel Plausible appraisal of likely outcome (e.g., likely disposition for one's own case) Comprehension of the implications of a guilty plea or plea bargain (i.e., the rights waived on entering a plea of guilty) Comprehension of the implications of proceeding pro se (e.g., the rights waived and the ramifications of the waiver) Capacity to make a reasoned choice about defense options (e.g., trial strategy, guilty plea, plea bargain, proceeding pro se, pleading insanity) without distortion attributable to mental illness (an ability to rationally apply knowledge to one's own case and make decisions)
Capacity to understand the adversarial nature of the proceedings	Understanding of the roles of courtroom personnel (i.e., judge, jury, prosecutor) Understanding of courtroom procedure (the basic sequence of trial events) Understanding of legal procedure (types of information that can be used as evidence, what is meant by an oath/pledge, how certain a judge or jury has to be to find one guilty)
Capacity to manifest appropriate courtroom behavior	Appreciation of appropriate courtroom behavior Capacity to manage one's emotions and behavior in the courtroom

(Continued)

Domain	Subdomain
Capacity to participate in trial	Capacity to track events as they unfold (not attributable to the effects of medication)
	Capacity to challenge witnesses (i.e., recognize distortions in witness testimony)
Capacity to testify relevantly	Capacity to manage one's emotional or communication difficulties
	Capacity to track oral questions and respond appropriately
Relationship with counsel	Recognition that counsel is an ally
	Appreciation of the attorney–client privilege
	Confidence in and trust in one's counsel
	Confidence in attorneys in general
	Particular relationship variables that may interfere with the specific attorney–client relationship (i.e., attorney skill in working with the client; problematic socioeconomic or demographic differences between counsel and client)
Medication effects on CST	Capacity to track proceedings, given sedation level on current medication
	Potentially detrimental effects of medication on the defendant's courtroom demeanor

Source: Adapted mainly from the work of Jennifer Skeem and colleagues (Skeem & Golding, 1998; Skeem, Golding, & Emke-Francis, 2004; Skeem, Golding, Cohn, & Berge, 1998) but with additions made from the *Fitness Interview Test– Revised* (Roesch, Zapf, & Eaves, 2006).

References

American Bar Association. (1989). *ABA criminal justice mental health standards*. Washington, DC: Author.

American Psychiatric Association. (2000). Diagnostic and statistical manual of mental disorders (Revised 4th ed.). Washington, DC: Author.

American Psychological Association. (2002). Ethical principles of psychologists and code of conduct. *American Psychologist, 57*, 1060–1073.

American Psychological Association. (2007). Record keeping guidelines. *American Psychologist, 62*, 993–1004.

Anderson, S. D., & Hewitt, J. (2002). The effect of competency restoration training on defendants with mental retardation found not competent to proceed. *Law and Human Behavior, 26*, 343–351.

Appelbaum, K. L. (1994). Assessing defendants with mental retardation. *Journal of Psychiatry and Law, 22*, 311–327.

Bagby, R., Nicholson, R., Rogers, R., & Nussbaum, D. (1992). Domains of competence to stand trial: A factor analytic study. *Law and Human Behavior, 16*, 491–506.

Bank, S. C., & Packer, I. K. (2007). Expert witness testimony: Law, ethics, and practice. In A. M. Goldstein (Ed.), *Forensic psychology: Emerging topics and expanding roles* (pp. 421–445). Hoboken, NJ: Wiley.

Bennett, G., & Kish, G. (1990). Incompetency to stand trial: Treatment unaffected by demographic variables. *Journal of Forensic Sciences, 35*, 403–412.

Bertman, L. J., Thompson, J. W., Jr., Waters, W. F., Estupinan-Kane, L., Martin, J. A., & Russell, L. (2003). Effect of an individualized treatment protocol on restoration of competency in pretrial forensic inpatients. *Journal of the American Academy of Psychiatry and Law, 31*, 27–35.

Blackstone, W. (1765). *Commentaries on the laws of England, Volume 1: Of the rights of persons*. Oxford, England: Clarendon Press. Reprinted in 1979 by the University of Chicago Press.

Blackstone, W. (1766). *Commentaries on the laws of England, Volume 2: Of the rights of things*. Oxford, England: Clarendon Press. Reprinted in 1979 by the University of Chicago Press.

Blackstone, W. (1768). *Commentaries on the laws of England, Volume 3: Of private wrongs*. Oxford, England: Clarendon Press. Reprinted in 1979 by the University of Chicago Press.

Blackstone, W. (1769). *Commentaries on the laws of England, Volume 4: Of public wrongs*. Oxford, England: Clarendon Press. Reprinted in 1979 by the University of Chicago Press.

Bonnie, R. J. (1992a). The competence of criminal defendant with mental retardation to participate in their own defense. *Journal of Criminal Law and Criminology, 81*, 419–446.

Bonnie, R. J. (1992b). The competence of criminal defendants: A theoretical reformulation. *Behavioral Sciences and the Law, 10,* 291–316.

Bonnie, R. J. (1993). The competence of criminal defendants: Beyond *Dusky* and *Drope. Miami Law Review, 47,* 539–601.

Bonnie, R. J., & Grisso, T. (2000). Adjudicative competence and youthful offenders. In T. Grisso & R. G. Schwartz (Eds.), *Youth on trial: A developmental perspective on juvenile justice* (pp. 73–103). Chicago, IL: University of Chicago Press.

Borum, R., & Grisso, T. (1995). Psychological test use in criminal forensic evaluations. *Professional Psychology: Research and Practice, 26,* 465–473.

Borum, R., & Grisso, T. (1996). Establishing standards for criminal forensic reports: An empirical analysis. *Bulletin of the American Academy of Psychiatry and the Law, 24,* 297–317.

Brakel, S. (1974). Presumption, bias, and incompetence in the criminal process. *Wisconsin Law Review,* pp. 1105–1130.

Brodsky, S. L. (1991). *Testifying in court: Guidelines and maxims for the expert witness.* Washington, DC: American Psychological Association.

Brodsky, S. L. (1999). *The expert expert witness: More maxims and guidelines for testifying in court.* Washington, DC: American Psychological Association.

Brodsky, S. L. (2004). *Coping with cross-examination and other pathways to effective testimony.* Washington, DC: American Psychological Association.

Bukatman, B. A., Foy, J. L., & DeGrazia, E. (1971). What is competency to stand trial? *American Journal of Psychiatry, 127,* 1225–1229.

Burt, R. A., & Morris, N. (1972). A proposal for the abolition of the incompetency plea. *University of Chicago Law Review, 40,* 66–95.

Carbonell, J., Heilbrun, K., & Friedman, F. (1992). Predicting who will regain trial competence: Initial promise unfulfilled. *Forensic Reports, 5,* 67–76.

Ciccone, J. R. (2007). Competence to stand trial and psychopathic disorders: Legal and clinical perspectives from the USA. In A. Felthous & H. Sass (Eds.), *International handbook of psychopathic disorders and the law: Law and policies,* Volume II (pp. 189–200). Hoboken, NJ: Wiley.

Cochrane, R. E., Grisso, T., & Frederick, R. I. (2001). The relationship between criminal charges, diagnoses, and psycholegal opinions among federal pretrial defendants. *Behavioral Sciences and the Law, 19,* 565–582.

Committee on Ethical Guidelines for Forensic Psychologists. (1991). Specialty guidelines for forensic psychologists. *Law and Human Behavior, 15,* 655–665.

Cooper, D. K., & Grisso, T. (1997). Five-year research update (1991–1995): Evaluations for competence to stand trial. *Behavioral Sciences and the Law, 15,* 347–364.

Cooper, V. G, & Zapf, P. A. (2003). Predictor variables in competency to stand trial decisions. *Law and Human Behavior, 27,* 423–436.

Cox, M. L., & Zapf, P. A. (2004). An investigation of discrepancies between mental health professionals and the courts in decisions about competency. *Law and Psychology Review, 28,* 109–132.

Cruise, K. R., & Rogers, R. (1998). An analysis of competency to stand trial: An integration of case law and clinical knowledge. *Behavioral Sciences and the Law, 16,* 35–50.

Cuneo, D., & Brelje, T. (1984). Predicting probability of attaining fitness to stand trial. *Psychological Reports, 55,* 35–39.

Daniel, A. E., & Menninger, K. (1983). Mentally retarded defendants: Competency and criminal responsibility. *American Journal of Forensic Psychiatry, 4,* 145–156.

Davis, D. L. (1985). Treatment planning for the patient who is incompetent to stand trial. *Hospital and Community Psychiatry, 36,* 268–271.

Edgerton, R. B. (1993). *The cloak of competence* (2nd ed.). Berkeley, CA: University of California Press.

Ellis, J. W., & Luckasson, R. A. (1985). Mentally retarded criminal defendants. *George Washington Law Review, 53,* 414–493.

Ericson, K., & Perlman, N. (2001). Knowledge of legal terminology and court proceedings in adults with developmental disabilities. *Law and Human Behavior, 25,* 529–545.

Everington, C. T. (1990). The Competence Assessment for Standing Trial for Defendants with Mental Retardation (CAST-MR): A validation study. *Criminal Justice* and *Behavior, 17,* 147–168.

Everington, C., & Dunn, C. (1995). A second validation study of The Competence Assessment for Standing Trial for Defendants with Mental Retardation (CAST-MR). *Criminal Justice and Behavior, 22,* 44–59.

Everington, C. T., Notario-Smull, H., & Horton, M. L. (2007). Can defendants with mental retardation successfully fake their performances on a test of competence to stand trial? *Behavioral Sciences and the Law, 25,* 545–560.

Ewing, C. P. (2003). Expert testimony: Law and practice. In A. M. Goldstein (Ed.), *Handbook of psychology: Forensic psychology* (Vol. 11, pp. 55–66). Hoboken, NJ: Wiley.

Farkas, G., DeLeon, P., & Newman, R. (1997). Sanity examiner certification: An evolving national agenda. *Professional Psychology: Research & Practice, 28,* 73–76.

Fitzgerald, J., Peszke, M., & Goodwin, R. (1978). Competency evaluations in Connecticut. *Hospital and Community Psychiatry, 29,* 450–453.

Gacono, C. B., Meloy, J. R., Sheppard, K., Speth, E., & Roske, A. (1995). A clinical investigation of malingering and psychopathy in hospitalized insanity acquittees. *Bulletin of the American Academy of Psychiatry and the Law, 23,* 387–397.

Gobert, J. J. (1973). Competency to stand trial: A pre- and post-*Jackson* analysis. *Tennessee Law Review, 40,* 659–688.

Golding, S. L. (1992). Studies of incompetent defendants: Research and social policy implications. *Forensic Reports, 5,* 77–83.

Golding, S. L., & Roesch, R. (1988). Competency for adjudication: An international analysis. In D. N. Weisstub (Ed.), *Law and mental health: International perspectives* (Vol. 4, pp. 73–109). Elmsford, NY: Pergamon Press.

Goldstein, A. M., & Burd, M. (1990). Role of delusions in trial competency evaluations: Case law and implications for forensic practice. *Forensic Reports, 3,* 361–386.

Greenberg, S., & Shuman, D. (1997). Irreconcilable conflict between therapeutic and forensic roles. *Professional Psychology: Research and Practice, 28,* 50–57

Grisso, T. (1986). *Evaluating competencies: Forensic assessment and instruments.* New York: Plenum.

Grisso, T. (1988). *Competency to stand trial evaluations: A manual for practice.* Sarasota, FL: Professional Resource Press.

Grisso, T. (2003). *Evaluating competencies: Forensic assessment and instruments* (2nd ed.). New York: Kluwer Academic/Plenum Publishers.

Grisso, T. (2005). *Evaluating juveniles' adjudicative competence: A guide for clinical practice.* Sarasota, FL: Professional Resource Press.

Grisso, T., Appelbaum, P. S., Mulvey, E., & Fletcher, K. (1995). The MacArther Treatment Competence Study, II: Measures of abilities related to competence to consent to treatment. *Law and Human Behavior, 19,* 127–148.

Grisso, T., Cocozza, J., Steadman, H., Fisher, W., & Greer, A. (1994). The organization of pretrial forensic evaluation services: A national profile. *Law and Human Behavior, 18,* 377–393.

Group for the Advancement of Psychiatry. (1974). *Misuse of psychiatry in the criminal courts: Competency to stand trial.* New York: Mental Health Materials Center.

Gutheil, T. G. (1998). *The psychiatrist as expert witness.* Washington, DC: American Psychiatric Press.

Hart, S. D., & Hare, R. D. (1992). Predicting fitness for trial: The relative power of demographic, criminal and clinical variables. *Forensic Reports, 5,* 53–54.

Heilbrun, K. (1992). The role of psychological testing in forensic assessment. *Law and Human Behavior, 16,* 257–272.

Heilbrun, K. (2001). *Principles of forensic mental health assessment.* New York: Kluwer Academic/Plenum Publishers.

Heilbrun, K., & Collins, S. (1995). Evaluations of trial competency and mental state at time of offense: Report characteristics. *Professional Psychology: Research and Practice, 26,* 61–67.

Heilbrun, K., Grisso, T., & Goldstein, A. M. (2008). *Foundations of forensic mental health assessment.* New York: Oxford University Press.

Heilbrun, K., Marczyk, G. R., & DeMatteo, D. (2002). *Forensic mental health assessment: A casebook.* New York: Oxford.

Heilbrun, K., Warren, J., & Picarello, K. (2003). Third-party information in forensic assessment. In A. M. Goldstein (Ed.), *Handbook of psychology: Forensic psychology* (Vol. 11, pp. 69–86). Hoboken, NJ: Wiley.

Heinze, M. C., & Vess, J. (2005). The relationship among malingering, psychopathy, and the MMPI-2 validity scales in maximum security forensic psychiatric inpatients. *Journal of Forensic Psychology Practice, 5*, 35–53.

Hess, A. K. (2006). Serving as an expert witness. In I. B. Weiner & A. K. Hess (Eds.), *The handbook of forensic psychology* (3rd ed., pp. 652–697). Hoboken, NJ: John Wiley & Sons.

Hoge, S., Bonnie, R., Poythress, N., & Monahan, J. (1992). Attorney–client decision making in criminal cases: Client competence and participation as perceived by their attorneys. *Behavioral Sciences and the Law, 10,* 385–394.

Hoge, S. K., Poythress, N., Bonnie, R. J., Monahan, J., Eisenberg, M., & Feucht-Haviar, T. (1997). The MacArthur adjudicative competence study: Diagnosis, psychopathology, and competence-related abilities. *Behavioral Sciences and the Law, 15,* 329–345.

Hubbard, K. L., & Zapf, P. A. (2003). The role of demographic, criminal, and psychiatric variables in examiners' predictions of restorability to competency to stand trial. *International Journal of Forensic Mental Health, 2,* 145–155.

Hubbard K. L, Zapf P. A., & Ronan K. A. (2003). Competency restoration: An examination of the differences between defendants predicted restorable and not restorable to competency. *Law and Human Behavior, 27,* 127–139.

James, D. V., Duffield, G., Blizard, R., & Hamilton, L. W. (2001). Fitness to plead: A prospective study of the inter-relationships between expert opinion, legal criteria and specific symptomatology. *Psychological Medicine, 31,* 139–150.

Kruh, I. & Grisso, T. (2009). *Evaluations of juveniles' competence to stand trial.* New York: Oxford University Press.

Kruh, I., Sullivan, L., & Dunham, J. (2001). *Respondent's attorney competency questionnaire.* State of Washington Department of Social and Health Services, Child Study and Treatment Center.

Laben, J. K., Kashgarian, M., Nessa, D. B., & Spencer, L. D. (1977). Reform from the inside: Mental health center evaluations of competency to stand trial. *Journal of Community Psychology, 5,* 52–62.

LaFortune, K., & Nicholson, R. (1995). How adequate are Oklahoma's mental health evaluations for determining competency in criminal proceedings? The bench and bar respond. *Journal of Psychiatry and Law, 23,* 231–262.

Martell, D. A., Rosner, R., & Harmon, R. B. (1994). Homeless mentally disordered defendants: Competency to stand trial and mental status findings. *Bulletin of the American Academy of Psychiatry and the Law, 22,* 289–295.

Melton, G. B., Petrila, J., Poythress, N. G., & Slobogin, C. (1987). *Psychological evaluations for the courts: A handbook for mental health professionals and lawyers.* New York: Guilford.

Melton, G. B., Petrila, J., Poythress, N. G., & Slobogin, C. (1997). *Psychological evaluations for the courts: A handbook for mental health professionals and lawyers* (2nd ed.). New York: Guilford.

Melton, G. B., Petrila, J., Poythress, N. G., & Slobogin, C. (2007). *Psychological evaluations for the courts: A handbook for mental health professionals and lawyers* (3rd ed.). New York: Guilford.

Melton, G., Weithorn, L., & Slobogin, C. (1987). *Community mental health centers and the courts: An evaluation of community-based forensic services.* Lincoln: University of Nebraska Press.

Miller, R. D. (2003). Criminal competence. In R. Rosner (Ed.), *Principles and practice of forensic psychiatry* (2nd ed., pp. 213–232). London: Arnold.

Morris, G. H., Haroun, A. M., & Naimark, D. (2004). Assessing competency competently: Toward a rational standard for competency-to-stand-trial assessments. *Journal of the American Academy of Psychiatry and Law, 32,* 231–45.

Morse, S. J. (1978). Law and mental health professionals: The limits of expertise. *Professional Psychology, 9,* 389–399.

Mossman, D. (2007). Predicting restorability of incompetent criminal defendants. *The Journal of the American Academy of Psychiatry and the Law, 35,* 34–43.

Mossman, D., Noffsinger, S. G., Ash, P., Frierson, R. L., Gerbasi, J., Hackett, M., Lewis, C. F., Pinals, D. A., Scott, C. L., Sieg, K. G., Wall, B. W., & Zonana, H. V. (2007). AAPL practice guideline for the forensic psychiatric evaluation of competence to stand trial. *Journal of the American Academy of Psychiatry and the Law, 35,* S3–S72.

Nicholson, R., Barnard, G., Robbins, L., & Hankins, G. (1994). Predicting treatment outcome for incompetent defendants. *Bulletin of the American Academy of Psychiatry and the Law, 22,* 367–377.

Nicholson, R., Briggs, S., & Robertson, H. (1988). Instruments for assessing competence to stand trial: How do they work? *Professional Psychology: Research and Practice, 19,* 383–394.

Nicholson, R. A., & Kugler, K. E. (1991). Competent and incompetent criminal defendants: A quantitative review of comparative research. *Psychological Bulletin, 109,* 355–370.

Nicholson, R., & McNulty, J. (1992). Outcome of hospitalization for defendants found incompetent to stand trial. *Behavioral Sciences and the Law, 10, 371–*383.

Nicholson, R., Robertson, H., Johnson, W. G., & Jensen, G. (1988). A comparison of instruments for assessing competence to stand trial. *Law and Human Behavior, 12,* 313–321.

Nottingham, E. J., & Mattson, R. E. (1981). A validation study of the Competency Screening Test. *Law and Human Behavior, 5,* 329–335.

Ogloff, J. R. P., & Roesch, R. (1992). Using community mental health centers to provide comprehensive mental health services to local jails. In J. R. P. Ogloff (Ed.), *Law and psychology: Broadening of the discipline* (pp. 241–260). Durham, NC: Carolina Academic Press.

Otto, R., Poythress, N., Edens, N., Nicholson, R., Monahan, J., Bonnie, R., Hoge, S., & Eisenberg, M. (1998). Psychometric properties of the MacArthur Competence Assessment Tool-Criminal Adjudication. *Psychological Assessment, 10,* 435–443.

Otto, R. K., Slobogin, C., & Greenberg, S. A. (2007). Legal and ethical issues in accessing and utilizing third-party information. In A. M. Goldstein (Ed.), *Forensic psychology: Emerging topics and expanding roles* (pp. 190–205). Hoboken, NJ: Wiley.

Pendleton, L. (1980). Treatment of persons found incompetent to stand trial. *American Journal of Psychiatry, 137,* 1098–1100.

Perlin, M. L. (1996). "Dignity was the first to leave": *Godinez v. Moran,* Colin Ferguson, and the trial of mentally disabled criminal defendants. *Behavioral Sciences and the Law, 14,* 61–81.

Petrella, R. C. (1992). Defendants with mental retardations in the forensic services system. In R. W. Conley, R. Luckasson, & G. N. Bouthilet (Eds.), *The criminal justice system and mental retardation* (pp. 79–96). Baltimore: Brookes.

Pinals, D. (2005). Where two roads met: Restoration of competence to stand trial from a clinical perspective. *New England Journal of Civil and Criminal Confinement, 31,* 81–108.

Poythress, N. G., Bonnie, R. J., Monahan, J., Otto, R. K., & Hoge, S. K. (2002). *Adjudicative competence: The MacArthur studies.* NY: Kluwer Academic/Plenum.

Poythress, N., & Stock, H. (1980). Competency to stand trial: A historical review and some new data. *Journal of Psychiatry and Law, 8,* 131–146.

Randolph, J., Hicks, T., & Mason, D. (1981). The Competence Screening Test: A replication and extension. *Criminal Justice and Behavior, 8,* 471–481.

Reich, J., & Wells, J. (1985). Psychiatric diagnosis and competency to stand trial. *Comprehensive Psychiatry, 26,* 421–432.

Reich, J., & Tookey, L. (1986). Disagreements between court and psychiatrist on competency to stand trial. *Journal of Clinical Psychiatry, 47,* 616–623.

Riley, S. E. (1998). Competency to stand trial adjudication: A comparison of female and male defendants. *Journal of the American Academy of Psychiatry and the Law, 26,* 223–240.

Robbins, E., Waters, J., & Herbert, P. (1997). Competency to stand trial evaluations: A study of actual practice in two states. *Journal of the American Academy of Psychiatry and Law, 25,* 469–483.

Robertson, A. J. (1925). *The laws of the kings of England: Edward to Henry I.* Cambridge, England: Cambridge University Press.

Roesch, R. (1995). Mental health interventions in pretrial jails. In G. Davies, S. Lloyd-Bostock, M. McMurran, & C. Wilson, (Eds.), *Psychology, law, and criminal justice: International developments in research and practice* (pp. 520–531). Oxford, England: Walter De Gruyter.

Roesch, R., & Golding, S. L. (1980). *Competency to stand trial.* Chicago, IL: University of Illinois Press.

Roesch, R., & Golding, S. L. (1985). The impact of deinstitutionalization. In D. P. Farrington & J. Gunn (Eds.), *Current research in forensic psychiatry and psychology: Aggression and dangerousness* (pp. 209–239). NY: Wiley.

Roesch, R., & Ogloff, J. R. P. (1996). Settings for providing civil and criminal mental health services. In B. D. Sales & S. A. Shah (Eds.), *Mental health and law: Research, policy and services* (pp. 191–218). Durham, NC: Carolina Academic Press.

Roesch, R., Ogloff, J. R. P., Hart, S. D., Dempster, R. J., Zapf, P. A., & Whittemore, K. E. (1997). The impact of Canadian Criminal Code changes on remands and assessments of competency to stand trial and criminal responsibility in British Columbia. *Canadian Journal of Psychiatry, 42,* 509–514.

Roesch, R., Zapf, P. A., Golding, S. L., & Skeem, J. (1999). Defining and assessing competency to stand trial. In I. B. Weiner & A. K. Hess (Eds.), *Handbook of forensic psychology* (2nd ed., pp. 327–349). New York: John Wiley and Sons.

Rogers, R. (1997). Introduction. In R. Rogers, (Ed.), *Clinical assessment of malingering and deception* (2nd ed., pp. 1–19). New York: Guilford.

Rogers, R. (2001). *Handbook of diagnostic and structured interviewing.* New York: Guilford.

Rogers, R., Grandjean, N., Tillbrook, C., Vitacco, M., & Sewell, K. (2001). Recent interview-based measures of competence to stand trial: A critical review augmented with research data. *Behavioral Sciences and the Law, 19,* 503–518.

Rogers, R., & Mitchell, C. N. (1991). *Mental health experts and the criminal courts: A handbook for lawyers and clinicians.* Scarborough, ON: Thompson.

Rosenfeld, B., & Ritchie, K. (1998). Competence to stand trial: Clinical reliability and the role of offense severity. *Journal of Forensic Sciences, 43,* 151–157.

Rosenfeld, B., & Wall, A. (1998). Psychopathology and competence to stand trial. *Criminal Justice and Behavior, 25,* 443–462.

Ryba, N. L., Cooper, V. G., & Zapf, P. A. (2003). Juvenile competence to stand trial evaluations: A survey of current practices and test usage among psychologists. *Professional Psychology: Research and Practice, 34,* 499–507.

Saldaña, D. (2001). *Cultural competency: A practical guide for mental health service providers.* Austin: Hogg Foundation for Mental Health, University of Texas at Austin.

Schlesinger, L. B. (2003). A case study involving competency to stand trial: Incompetent defendant, incompetent examiner, or 'malingering by proxy'? *Psychology, Public Policy, and Law, 9,* 381–399.

Schreiber, J. (1978). Assessing competency to stand trial: A case study of technology diffusion in four states. *Bulletin of the American Academy of Psychiatry and the Law, 6,* 439–457.

Shatin, L. (1979). Brief form of the Competence Screening Test for mental competence to stand trial. *Journal of Clinical Psychology, 35,* 464–467.

Siegel, A. M., & Elwork, A. (1990). Treating incompetence to stand trial. *Law and Human Behavior, 14,* 57–65.

Skeem, J. L., & Golding, S. L. (1998). Community examiners' evaluations of competence to stand trial: Common problems and suggestions for improvement. *Professional Psychology: Research and Practice, 29,* 357–367.

Skeem, J., Golding, S. L., Cohn, N., & Berge, G. (1998). Logic and reliability of evaluations of competence to stand trial. *Law and Human Behavior, 22,* 519–547.

Skeem, J., Golding, S. L., & Emke-Francis, P. (2004). Assessing adjudicative competency: Using legal and empirical principles to inform practice. In W. O'Donohue & E. Levensky (Eds.), *Handbook of forensic psychology: Resource for mental health and legal professionals* (pp. 175–211). NY: Academic Press.

Slobogin, C. (1989). The "ultimate issue" issue. *Behavioral Sciences and the Law, 7,* 259–266.

Steadman, H. J. (1979). *Beating a rap? Defendants found incompetent to stand trial.* Chicago: University of Chicago Press.

Tseng, W., Matthews, D., Elwyn, T. S. (2004). *Cultural competence in forensic mental health: A guide for psychiatrists, psychologists, and attorneys.* New York: Brunner/Routledge.

Tsushima, W. T., & Anderson, R. M., Jr. (1996). *Mastering expert testimony: A courtroom handbook for mental health professionals.* Mahwah, NJ: Erlbaum.

Ustad, K. L., Rogers, R., Sewell, K. W., & Guarnaccia, C. A. (1996). Restoration of competency to stand trial: Assessment with the Georgia Court Competency Test and the Competency Screening Test. *Law and Human Behavior, 20,* 131–146.

Viljoen, J. L., Roesch, R., Ogloff, J. R. P., & Zapf, P. A. (2003). The role of Canadian psychologists in conducting fitness and criminal responsibility evaluations. *Canadian Psychology, 44,* 369–381.

Viljoen, J. L., Roesch, R., & Zapf, P. A. (2002a). Interrater reliability of the Fitness Interview Test across four professional groups. *Canadian Journal of Psychiatry, 47,* 945–952.

Viljoen, J. L., Roesch, R., & Zapf, P. A. (2002b). An examination of the relationship between competency to stand trial, competency to waive interrogation rights, and psychopathology. *Law and Human Behavior, 26,* 481–506.

Viljoen, J. L., & Zapf, P. A. (2002). Fitness to stand trial evaluations: A comparison of referred and non-referred defendants. *International Journal of Forensic Mental Health, 1,* 127–138.

Viljoen, J. L., Zapf, P. A., & Roesch, R. (2003). Diagnosis, current psychiatric symptoms, and the ability to stand trial. *Journal of Forensic Psychology Practice, 3*, 23–37.

Warren J. I., Fitch, W. L., Dietz, P. E., & Rosenfeld, B. D. (1991). Criminal offense, psychiatric diagnosis, and psychological opinion: An analysis of 894 pretrial referrals. *Bulletin of American Academy of Psychiatry and Law, 20*, 63–69.

Warren, J. I., Rosenfeld, B., Fitch, W. L., & Hawk, G. (1997). Forensic mental health clinical evaluation: An analysis of interstate and intersystemic differences. *Law and Human Behavior, 21*, 377–390.

Weiner, I. B. (2006). Writing forensic reports. In I. B. Weiner & A. K. Hess (Eds.), *The handbook of forensic psychology* (3ʳᵈ ed., pp. 631–651). Hoboken, NJ: John Wiley & Sons.

Whittemore, K. E., Ogloff, J. R. P., & Roesch, R. (1997). An investigation of competence to participate in legal proceedings in Canada. *Canadian Journal of Psychiatry, 42*, 869–875.

Zapf, P. A. (2002). *A comparison of competency statutes.* Unpublished manuscript. Available from the author.

Zapf, P. A., Hubbard, K. L., Cooper, V. G., Wheeles, M. C., & Ronan, K. A. (2004). Have the courts abdicated their responsibility for determination of competency to stand trial to clinicians? *Journal of Forensic Psychology Practice, 4*, 27–44.

Zapf, P. A., & Roesch, R. (1998). Fitness to stand trial: Characteristics of remands since the 1992 Criminal Code amendments. *Canadian Journal of Psychiatry, 43*, 287–293.

Zapf, P. A., & Roesch, R. (2001). A comparison of the MacCAT-CA and the FIT for making determinations of competency to stand trial. *International Journal of Law and Psychiatry, 24*, 81–92.

Zapf, P. A., & Roesch, R. (2005a). Competency to stand trial: A guide for evaluators. In I. B. Weiner & A. K. Hess (Eds.), *Handbook of forensic psychology* (3ʳᵈ ed., pp. 305–331). New York: Wiley.

Zapf, P. A., & Roesch, R. (2005b). An investigation of the construct of competence: A comparison of the FIT, the MacCAT-CA, and the MacCAT-T. *Law and Human Behavior, 29*, 229–252.

Zapf, P. A., Roesch, R., & Viljoen, J. L. (2001) Assessing fitness to stand trial: The utility of the Fitness Interview Test (revised edition). *Canadian Journal of Psychiatry, 46*, 426–432.

Zapf, P. A., Skeem, J. L., & Golding, S. L. (2005). Factor structure and validity of the MacArthur Competence Assessment Tool—Criminal Adjudication. *Psychological Assessment, 17*, 433–445.

Zapf, P. A., & Viljoen, J. L. (2003). Issues and considerations regarding the use of assessment instruments in the evaluation of competency to stand trial. *Behavioral Sciences and the Law, 21*, 351–367.

Ziskin, J., & Faust, D. (1995). *Coping with psychiatric and psychological testimony.* Beverly Hills, CA: Law and Psychology Press.

Tests and Specialized Tools

BPRS: Brief Psychiatric Rating Scale (Overall & Gorham, 1962)

CADCOMP: Computer-Assisted Determination of Competence to Proceed (Barnard, Thompson, Freeman, Robbins, Gies, & Hankins, 1991)

CAI: Competency Assessment Instrument (Laboratory of Community Psychiatry, 1973; McGarry & Curran, 1973)

CAST*MR: Competence Assessment for Standing Trial for Defendants with Mental Retardation (Everington & Luckasson, 1992)

CST: Competency Screening Test (Lipsitt, Lelos, & McGarry, 1971)

ECST-R: Evaluation of Competency to Stand Trial–Revised (Rogers, Tillbrook, & Sewell, 2004)

FIT: Fitness Interview Test (Roesch, Webster, & Eaves, 1984)

FIT-R: Fitness Interview Test–Revised (Roesch, Zapf, Eaves, & Webster, 1998; Roesch, Zapf, & Eaves, 2006)

GCCT: Georgia Court Competency Test (Wildman et al., 1978)

GCCT-R: Georgia Court Competency Test-Revised (Johnson & Mullett, 1987)

GCCT-MSH: Georgia Court Competency Test–Mississippi State Hospital Revision (Wildman, White, & Brandenburg, 1990)

IFI: Interdisciplinary Fitness Interview (Golding, Roesch, & Schreiber, 1984)

IFI-R: Interdisciplinary Fitness Interview–Revised (Golding, 1993)

JSAT: Jail Screening Assessment Tool (Nicholls, Roesch, Olley, Ogloff, & Hemphill, 2005)

MacCAT-CA: MacArthur Competence Assessment Tool–Criminal Adjudication (Hoge, Bonnie, Poythress, & Monahan, 1999; Poythress et al., 1999)

M-FAST: Miller Forensic Assessment of Symptoms Test (Miller, 1995)

MMPI-2: Minnesota Multiphasic Personality Inventory-2 (Hathaway & McKinley, 1989)

PCL-R: Hare Psychopathy Checklist–Revised (Hare, 1991, 2003)

PCL: SV: Hare Psychopathy Checklist: Screening Version (Hart, Cox, & Hare, 1995)

PPI: Psychopathic Personality Inventory (Lilienfeld & Andrews, 1996)

SCID-P: Structured Clinical Interview for DSM-III-R–Patient Edition (Spitzer, Williams, Gibbon, & First, 1990)

SIRS: Structured Interview of Reported Symptoms (Rogers, Bagby, & Dickens, 1992)

TOMM: Test of Memory Malingering (Tombaugh, 1996)

VIP: Validity Indicator Profile (Frederick, 1997)

WAIS-R: Wechsler Adult Intelligence Scale–Revised (Wechsler, 1981)

References for Tests and Specialized Tools

Barnard, G. W., Thompson, J. W., Freeman, W. C., Robbins, L., Gies, D., & Hankins, G. (1991). Competency to stand trial: Description and initial evaluation of a new computer-assisted assessment tool (CADCOMP). *Bulletin of the American Academy of Psychiatry and the Law, 19,* 367–381.

Everington, C. T., & Luckasson, R. (1992). *Competence assessment for standing trial for defendants with mental retardation.* Ohio: IDS Publishing Corporation.

Frederick, R. I. (1997). *Validity Indicator Profile (VIP) manual.* Minneapolis, MN: NCS Pearson.

Golding, S. L., (1993). *Interdisciplinary Fitness Interview–Revised: A training manual.* Unpublished monograph from State of Utah Division of Mental Health.

Golding, S. L., Roesch, R., & Schreiber, J. (1984). Assessment and conceptualization of competency to stand trial: Preliminary data on the Interdisciplinary Fitness Interview. *Law and Human Behavior, 8,* 321–334.

Hare, R. D. (1991). *Hare Psychopathy Checklist–Revised (PCL-R).* Toronto, ON: Multi-Health Systems.

Hare, R. D. (2003). *Hare Psychopathy Checklist–Revised (PCL-R) technical manual (2nd ed.).* Toronto, Ontario, Canada: Multi-Health Systems.

Hart, S. D., Cox, D. N., & Hare, R. D. (1995). *Hare Psychopathy Checklist: Screening Version (PCL:SV) technical manual.* Toronto, Ontario, Canada: Multi-Health Systems.

Hathaway, S. R., & McKinley, J. C. (1989). Manual for the Minnesota Multiphasic Personality Inventory-2 (MMPI-2). Minneapolis, MN: University of Minnesota Press.

Hoge, S. K., Bonnie, R. J., Poythress, N., & Monahan, J. (1999). *The MacArthur Competence Assessment Tool–Criminal Adjudication.* Odessa, FL: Psychological Assessment Resources.

Johnson, W. G., & Mullett, N. (1987). Georgia Court Competency Test–R. In M. Hersen & A. S. Bellack (Eds.), *Dictionary of behavioral assessment techniques.* New York: Pergamon Press.

Laboratory of Community Psychiatry, Harvard Medical School. (1973). *Competency to stand trial and mental illness* (DHEW Publication No. ADM77–103). Rockville, MD: Department of Health, Education and Welfare.

Lilienfeld, S. O., & Andrews, B. P. (1996). Development and preliminary validation of a self-report measures of psychopathic personality traits in noncriminal populations. *Journal of Personality Assessment, 66,* 488–524.

Lipsitt, P., Lelos, D., & McGarry, A. L. (1971). Competency for trial: A screening instrument. *American Journal of Psychiatry, 128,* 105–109.

McGarry, A. L., & Curran, W. J. (1973). *Competency to stand trial and mental illness.* Rockville, MD: National Institute of Mental Health.

Miller, H. A. (1995). *Miller Forensic Assessment of Symptoms Test (M-FAST) professional manual.* Odessa, FL: Psychological Assessment Resources.

Nicholls, T. L., Roesch, R., Olley, M. C., Ogloff, J. R. P., & Hemphill, J. F. (2005). *Jail Screening Assessment Tool (JSAT): Guidelines for mental health screening in jails.* Burnaby, BC: Mental Health, Law, and Policy Institute, Simon Fraser University.

Overall, J. E., & Gorham, D. R. (1962). The Brief Psychiatric Rating Scale. *Psychological Reports, 10,* 799–812.

Poythress, N. G., Nicholson, R. A., Otto, R. K., Edens, J. F., Bonnie, R. J., Monahan, J., & Hoge, S. K. (1999). *The MacArthur Competence Assessment Tool–Criminal Adjudication.* Odessa, FL: Psychological Assessment Resources.

Robey, A. (1965). Criteria for competency to stand trial: A checklist for psychiatrists. *American Journal of Psychiatry, 122,* 616–623.

Roesch, R., Webster, C. D., & Eaves, D. (1984). *The Fitness Interview Test: A method for examining fitness to stand trial.* Toronto, Ontario, Canada: Research Report of the Centre of Criminology, University of Toronto.

Roesch, R., Zapf, P. A., Eaves, D., & Webster, C. D. (1998). *Fitness Interview Test (Revised edition).* Burnaby, British Columbia, Canada: Mental Health, Law and Policy Institute, Simon Fraser University.

Roesch, R. Zapf, P. A., & Eaves, D. (2006). *Fitness Interview Test–Revised: A structured interview for assessing competency to stand trial.* Sarasota, FL: Professional Resource Press.

Rogers, R., Bagby, R. M., & Dickens, S. E. (1992). *Structured Interview of Reported Symptoms (SIRS) and professional manual.* Odessa, FL: Psychological Assessment Resources.

Rogers, R., Tillbrook, C. E., & Sewell, K. W. (2004). *Evaluation of Competency to Stand Trial–Revised professional manual.* Lutz, FL: Psychological Assessment Resources.

Spitzer, R. L., Williams, J. B. W., Gibbon, M., & First, M. B. (1990). *Structured Clinical Interview for DSM-III-R–Patient Edition* (SCID-P, Version 1.0). Washington, DC: American Psychiatric Press.

Tombaugh, T. N. (1996). *Test of Memory Malingering (TOMM) manual.* Toronto, ON: Multi-Health Systems.

Wechsler, D. (1981). *Wechsler Adult Intelligence Scale – Revised.* New York: The Psychological Corporation.

Wildman, R. W., Batchelor, E. S., Thompson, I., Nelson, F. R., Moore, J. T., Patterson, M. E., & de Laosa, M. (1978). *The Georgia Court Competency Test: An attempt to develop a rapid, quantitative measure of fitness for trial.* Unpublished manuscript, Forensic Services Division, Central State Hospital, Milledgeville, GA.

Wildman, R. W., II, White, P. A., & Brandenburg, C. A. (1990). The Georgia Court Competency Test: The base rate problem. *Perceptual and Motor Skills, 70,* 1055–1058.

Cases and Statutes

Cooper v. Oklahoma, 116 S. Ct. 1373 (1996).

Criminal Code of Canada, R. S. C., C-46 (1985).

Criminal Code of Canada, R. S. C., C. C-46. (1992).

Drope v. Missouri, 420 U. S. 162 (1975).

Dusky v. United States, 362 U. S. 402 (1960).

Estelle v. Smith, 451 U. S. 454 (1981).

Godinez v. Moran, 113 S. Ct. 2680 (1993).

Indiana v. Edwards, 554 U. S. ___ (2008).

Jackson v. Indiana, 406 U. S. 715 (1972).

Jenkins v. United States, 307 F. 2d. 637 (1962).

Miles v. Stainer, 108 F. 3d 1109, 1112–13 (9th Cir. 1997).

Pate v. Robinson, 383 U. S. 375 (1966).

Riggins v. Nevada, 504 U. S. 127 (1992).

Sell v. United States, 539 U. S. 166 (2003).

Sieling v. Eyman, 478 F. 2d. 211 (1973).

Tarasoff v. Regents of the University of California, 17 Cal. 3d. 425 (1976).

Utah Code Annotated §77–15–1 et seq. (1994).

Utah Code Annotated §77–15–5 et seq. (2002).

United States v. Duhon, 104 F. Supp. 2d. 663 (2000).

United States v. Lawrence, 26 F. Cas. 887 (D.C. Cir. 1835).

Wieter v. Settle, 193 F. Supp. 318 (W. D. Mo. 1961).

Wilson v. United States, 391 F. 2d. 460 (1968).

Youtsey v. United States, 97 F. 937 (6th Cir., 1899).

Key Terms

adjudicative competence: a newer term used for CST as it more accurately reflects the need of defendants to meaningfully participate in all stages of the adjudication process, not just at trial. *See also* competence to stand trial.

civil commitment: legally mandated psychiatric treatment based on specific criteria, usually including imminent risk of harm to self, risk of harm to others, and/or an inability to maintain adequate self-care.

competence restoration: intervention services aimed at establishing competence in a defendant found incompetent to stand trial, so that the adjudication process can go forward; based on the notion that psychotic defendants were once competent and can be "restored" to competence if the psychosis is diminished.

criminal responsibility: also known as insanity; refers to the mental status of the defendant at the time of the offense and is a defense that takes into consideration the ability of the defendant to understand the nature, quality, and wrongfulness of his actions.

competence to proceed: a newer term used for CST as it more accurately reflects the need of defendants to meaningfully participate in all stages of the adjudication process, not just at trial. *See also* competence to stand trial.

competence to stand trial (CST): a legal doctrine that requires meaningful participation of criminal defendants in their defense at various stages of the proceedings by requiring that defendants possess specific relevant abilities (i.e., understanding, appreciation, reasoning, assisting counsel, and decision making).

court-ordered evaluations: evaluations that are ordered by and "owned by" the court. Therefore, the court controls access to its contents through its own distribution practices or through statutes that direct the examiner about how to make those distributions.

cross-examination: testimony provided in response to questioning by the attorney who did not call the witness; more likely to take on an adversarial tone.

direct examination: testimony provided in response to questioning by the attorney who called the witness; more likely to be conducted in a supportive tone.

***Dusky* standard:** the standard for competence that was delineated in *Dusky v. United States* (1960), wherein a defendant must have a rational as well as factual understanding of the proceedings and be able to consult with counsel with a reasonable degree of rational understanding.

***ex parte* evaluations:** evaluations that are conducted on behalf of one of the attorneys within the context of being retained by that attorney. The results of the evaluation are typically shared with that attorney only, to be used at the discretion of the retaining attorney and as specified in law.

forensic assessment instruments (FAIs): structured quantitative interview tools designed for focused assessment of the functional legal abilities of direct relevance to legal questions.

forensically relevant instruments: psychological tests or instruments that assist in evaluating characteristics or conditions that, although not the focus of legal inquiry, might be considered in a forensic evaluation (e.g., intelligence tests, tests of malingering).

functional assessment of competency: an evaluation and description of the degree of congruence or incongruence between a defendant's competence-related abilities and the contextual demands of his case.

idiographic: data obtained through the investigation of one individual, usually the individual under consideration.

Incompetent to Stand Trial (IST): a legal finding in which a given defendant is identified as lacking in the abilities necessary to meaningfully participate in a relevant stage(s) of the proceedings.

informed consent: an individual's consent for another person to engage in intervention that would otherwise constitute an invasion of the individual's privacy, after the individual has been fully informed of the nature and consequences of the proposed action, is competent to consent, and consents voluntarily. Informed consent is not necessary on court-ordered or statutorily mandated evaluations in criminal or delinquency cases, or when authorized by legal counsel for the individual.

nomothetic: data obtained through the investigation of groups.

notification of rights: an explanation to the defendant about the conditions and limits of confidentiality inherent in the evaluation; the notification is often memorialized in writing.

pro se: Latin for "for self" and referring to representing oneself in a court proceeding without an attorney.

qualifying the expert: the process of expert testimony through which the court determines if an examiner is qualified to be admitted as an expert witness in the case at hand.

response style: the subtle or overt motivational approach used by an examinee during an evaluation that can significantly impact the data obtained. For example, some examinees may respond with full honesty and full effort, some may distort the results in an effort to appear a certain way, and others may put forth minimal effort in their responses.

threshold for questioning competence: the point at which questions about defendant's competence are significant enough to warrant a competence evaluation; generally a low threshold.

ultimate legal opinion: the legal determination to be made by the court regarding the issue before the judge (e.g., whether the individual should be civilly committed, whether the individual is competent to stand trial).

Index

About the Authors

Patricia A. Zapf, PhD, is currently associate professor in the Department of Psychology at John Jay College of Criminal Justice, the City University of New York. She is the associate editor of the *Encyclopedia of Psychology and Law* and an associate editor of *Law and Human Behavior*. She was appointed Fellow of the American Psychological Association in 2006 for outstanding contributions to the field of psychology and law. She has published over 60 articles and chapters, mainly on the assessment of criminal competencies. In addition to her research and publishing, she serves as a consultant to various criminal justice and policy organizations and maintains a private practice in forensic assessment. She received her doctoral degree in clinical forensic psychology from Simon Fraser University in Canada in 1999.

Ronald Roesch, PhD, is professor of psychology and director of the Mental Health, Law, and Policy Institute at Simon Fraser University. He served as president of the American Psychology-Law Society (APLS), and is president-elect of the International Association of Forensic Mental Health Services. He was editor of the journals *Law and Human Behavior* and the *International Journal of Forensic Mental Health,* and is currently the acting editor of *Psychology, Public Policy, and Law.* His book with Dr. Stephen Golding, *Competency to Stand Trial,* won a merit award in the American Bar Association Gavel Awards Competition. Dr. Roesch remains interested in research focusing on competency issues for both adult and juvenile offenders, and is also involved in studies of jail/prison mental health assessment, and youth violence.